30 DAYS TO
Unstoppable

BE THE DREAM
MADE VISIBLE

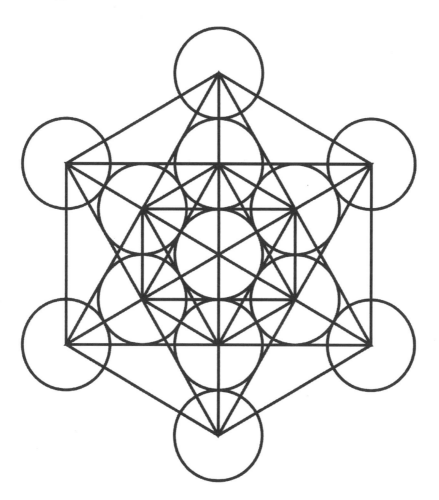

WHITNEY FREYA

Praise for
30 DAYS to Unstoppable

"In a time of undeniable transformation, *30 Days to Unstoppable* feels like a truth map back to our deepest knowing of self and what's possible when we're willing to move past fear and dream our wildest dreams alive. Whitney has offered us such a gift by sharing her wisdom here."

—FLORA BOWLEY, Painter, Pioneer, Permission-giver, Author of *Brave Intuitive Painting* and *Creative Revolution*

"*30 days to Unstoppable* is a must have book that helps you remember that you are the keeper of your dreams. Whitney Freya's words give you the tools and secret codes for deep transformation on your journey to a life fulfilled. I am so inspired by all the wisdom in this book. This is the ultimate guide for teaching high vibrational beings how to take care of themselves, so that they may thrive and live an empowered life filled with joy, grace and creativity."

—DR. MARIE MBOUNI,
Consciousness Coach,
Shaman, Speaker

"Whitney Freya's *30 Days to Unstoppable* guides you through a sacred process of connecting with Source. Energy is everything. Her artistic exercises will assist you in getting your energy aligned with Source and with your desires."

—LEAH GUZMAN, Artist and Art Therapist

"*30 Days to Unstoppable* gives me the greatest feeling of coming home within myself realising that I have all the tools within me to create my own life! This book is pure love and magic! It is the icing on the cake I needed to move on with my life knowing and believing! This is what the 30 days of Unstoppable did with me! I am thankful that you shared your knowledge and wisdom to help me and others to find their love, ease and peace! And if there would still come a moment where I feel myself disconnected from the whole, I can always take the book and read myself on track again! For me it is like a course in miracles!"

—ISTA ZELOU, Artist

"It is so very obvious to me that Whitney Freya has lived and does live everything that she shares in this very powerful and transformative book. Reading Whitney's book and hearing her story has changed my consciousness."

—**JEFF KRISMAN,** Host of ONEConsciousness Deep Conversations podcast

"*30 Days to Unstoppable* speaks to the heart of all of humanity at a time when we so deeply need its guidance. This book is the soulful companion you must have if you are on the journey of moving from 3D to 5D consciousness."

—**SHEREE KEYS,** Author of *The Release Pathways* and owner of the Austin Emotional Clearing Institute

"It's time to remember our magick. Whitney Freya shows how to use sacred geometry to align with the unstoppable force of life and harness it. *30 Days to Unstoppable* is perfectly channeled for this time."

—**AMBER KUILEIMAILANI BONNICI,** Founder of Woman Unleashed

"It is obvious to us all that this moment we find ourselves in calls for new thinking and new vision. We are all looking for a deeper sense of meaning in our time here. Whitney serves as a master guide for the seeker but does not just offer us knowledge. With *30 Days to Unstoppable,* she gives you clear, profound steps to actualize who we are meant to be in this most sacred time."

—**MARCUS WHITNEY,** Author of *Create and Orchestrate*

"Whitney is pure magic. She has the ability to create and share things in a way that leaves you feeling inspired and wanting more. Being in her energy feels otherworldly. She is the embodiment of the Unstoppable Dream!"

—**SUZANNE HANNA,** Founder and creator of The Wilderness Walk, Founder of Global Healing Collective

Praise for
30 DAYS to Unstoppable

"*30 Days to Unstoppable: BE the DREAM Made Visible* will be a thrill for your soul! Everyone deserves to know they are an infinite vibrational being and Whitney is a true leader in this world. Whitney guides you through a beautiful practice that will take you from a three dimensional perspective of your world, to one where your true unlimited potential is released. Thank you Whitney for sharing your gift of this expanded awareness with all of us here. Your work is incredibly valuable for the future vision of our world!"

—JANICE GALLANT, B.ED, Author and founder of The Creation Guild

"Whitney's words in *30 Days to Unstoppable* are more than a meditation or a journey. They are an activation sparking a deep knowing of who we really are as infinite beings. She has once again created a process that awakens the truth within. Now more than ever, we need Whitney's magic and guidance, because creating a new earth requires that we each start from within."

—TAMMY ROTH, PHD, Psychotherapist and Author of *High Bottom - Letting Go of Vodka & Chardonnay* and *New Bottom - Turning the Other Cheek*

"I am unstoppable! Exploring the spheres of wellness changed the vision of my future and provided the vibrational link between co-creation and the courage to leave my corporate career and start my own business."

—KIM SALES, Artist and Creatively Fit Coach

"The unstoppable dream process in *30 Days to Unstoppable* felt like a safety blanket wrapping me in a high vibration at a time when the world was truly in chaos. It allowed me to step back and observe the patterns I had been falling into and to re-choose the path my soul was calling me to follow. The greatest change for me in following the unstoppable dream process has been self love, specifically learning to listen to and love my body. Since following the process I've begun to reconnect with my body at a deeper level from which I disconnected in my mid teens. I've let go of stories around diet, I eat intuitively and my body has responded by letting go of weight it was holding to 'protect' me. This process is never ending, each time I visit another sphere of wellness something else shifts towards the path of my soul's calling."

—ANGELA MURRAY, CREATIVE GUIDE

"*30 Days to Unstoppable* is the must-read book for anyone who wants to live into their dreams. No matter where you are in your journey to embrace your creativity and live authentically, Whitney Freya's words and inspiration will help you live a life full of love, compassion, courage, and gratitude. With this book, you will help you to thrive and become unstoppable."

—TERRI L. RUSS, Saint Mary's College, Notre Dame, Indiana

"Whitney delivers beautiful, sacred meditations that create an amazing energy expansion for our journey of discovery, both inwards and outwards. I love the concept of using Metatron's cube for the expansion/experience. Thank you Whitney for creating the sacred space for personal development."

—LOIS WARNOCK, Spiritual Psychic Artist, Medium, and Coach

FLOWER *of* LIFE PRESS

Published by Flower of Life Press™
Old Saybrook, CT
Astara Jane Ashley, *Publisher*
floweroflifepress.com

Cover and interior design by Astara Jane Ashley

Art by Whitney Freya

Library of Congress Control Number: Available Upon Request

ISBN-13: 978-1-7349730-7-5
Printed in the United States of America

This is for you

… who believe in magic.

… who have always known life is extraordinary.

… who are devoted to embodying your most authentic Self.

… who envision a world that honors interconnectedness,
while celebrating diversity.

… who are learning to be more and more proud of your idealistic nature.

… who are dreamers.

… who are, in effect, holding space for what's possible for a
humanity that chooses love.

… who want to step into life each day bathed in a sense of union with the
eARTh below your feet and the stars above your head.

… who are ready for change.

And so it is.

Contents

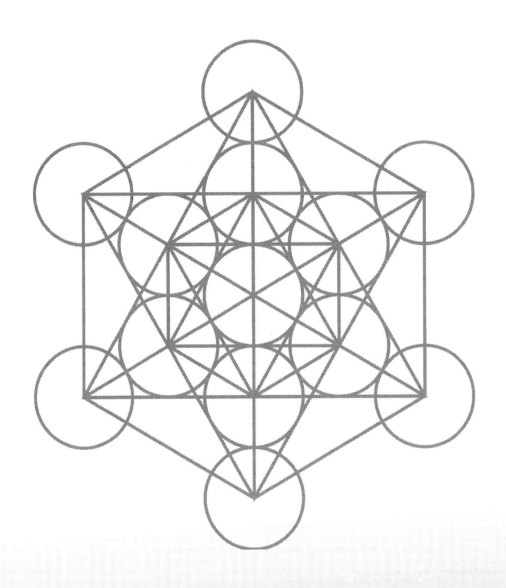

A Channeled Message

There was a time long, long ago, and then there is a time far into your future, perhaps not so far away, depending on the rate at which you accept this invitation, when you remembered union.

You understood the truth of connection.

There was no sense of separation.

You danced in circles as mother earth spun around the sun.

When it rained, you got wet.

When it snowed, you allowed mother earth to shelter you.

You built pyramids and temples that reflected the dance of the stars, the grand design of all existence mirrored for you in the dark skies, punctuated by beads of light.

Today you are remembering.

This remembrance is partly inspired by the state of your modern world, partly inspired by the disheartening and even frightening reality you've created that surrounds you.

You have reached a precipice, and from this vantage point you see clearly that continuing to live life as it has been lived up until now is no longer sustainable.

It's not sustainable at a material, emotional, or energetic level. The external world is, not randomly, guiding you within to upgrade the way you interpret, the way your process, and the way you create your life. It is this journey within where you will discover and remember union.

Your external reality reflects your internal reality.

Your external reality is a reflection of forgetting that one can only feel safe, secure, and loved when you nurture those feelings within you and for you.

How you think about your life and the realities you create within your mind—your stories, ideas, and inner dialogue—is ready to be remade. Now, your true quest is to expand your possibilities and break through to new levels of consciousness.

The truth is that you have everything you need within. As your external world becomes more unstable and the old ways of doing life on this planet transform, the peace and security you seek will come from within you. And because you learn to generate these feelings, these positive feelings will **attune you to a new level of personal power.**

Your physical being is energy. You know this now. Your science has proven it, and your logical mind can grasp it. Now you are being invited into a process that will enable you to receive all the guidance and security that you desire. You are being reminded how to cultivate a frequency that allows you, your life, your thoughts, and your dreams to align with that which is wanting to come through you.

What wants to come through you is love and the new earth.

What wants to come through you is a reality in which humanity is guided by love rather than fear.

You're now ready to let go of the beliefs that have led to cultural and societal separation. Soon the belief that anyone, any group or country, has to defend themselves with missiles and drones from other members of your human family will seem foreign and childish. You are ready to invest your "money energy" in life elements that create empowered children, restore the balance between humanity and the earth, and provide equal opportunity for all. You are prepared to create a modern reality that is aligned with the butterfly effect: that none of you exist independent of the other, that you are all one... period.

The process in this book will elevate your frequency and raise the vibration of the energy within and surrounding you so that the only ideas that can find harmony and residence will be those that are resonant with your frequency. You will align with a frequency that is compassionate, courageous, and loving, and these vibrations will yield a reality that inspires your gratitude.

As you read this book, it will be a remembrance more than a lesson.

Your existence is a union of matter and energy, stardust, and consciousness.

You are the physical, animated by the field of pure potentiality.

When your eyes light up, it is a reflection of the expansiveness of the stars.

You are meant to channel dreams and to create dreams into your reality, because they are not merely your dreams. They are the breakthroughs being given to humanity by a higher level of consciousness, to support and complete your journey from fear to love, from separation to oneness, from force to power, from domination to unity.

Thank you for receiving and for allowing this process time and space in your life.

You will feel rewarded and your future reality will be influenced, and you will celebrate life anew.

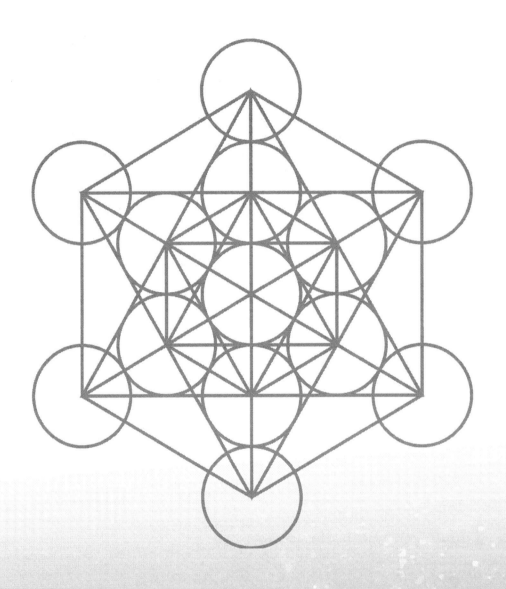

Introduction

BY WHITNEY FREYA

I'd like to introduce you to a new sense of personal security. We all know how unexpected events have rocked our world, and there is no longer a normal. Nothing is as we thought it would be, which can be tremendously unsettling, stressful, and worrisome.

We used to think insurance policies or investment accounts would provide us with the security we crave. But now we know that change is rampant—and we can no longer count on the way things used to be as we look ahead.

What to do?

I asked, "What are the basics that we need to live a happy, fulfilled life?" As humans, we are so good at complicating life, right? And I sensed there was a simpler way.

The answers came as I received a new kind of insurance policy—a personal meditation practice that created a protective bubble within and around me. It was like a map to happiness!

This was in 2019. Over the next several months, I was shown how we could follow a different pathway to our happiest life. The elements of the journey revealed themselves to me via a series of ah-ha moments. First, I was reminded that everything is energy. Then, I understood if we focused on high vibrational energies, we would become higher vibrational beings. Since *like attracts like* in the world of energy, high vibrational beings only attract more high vibrational energy. If we are immersed in and surrounded by high vibrational energy, how can our lives be anything *but* high vibration?

The kicker is this: As a high vibrational being, when you are given a dream and asked to co-create it into reality, you can choose to be *unstoppable*. With the support of all the high vibrational energy available to you, you have become the dream made visible—the unstoppable co-creator of the dream wanting to be made visible.

In January 2020, I described this state of being to my students as a type of Noah's ark. When we vibrate at a high frequency, anything coming into our experience has to match it or else raise our vibration to spend any time with us.

When we are vibrating at a high frequency, we can only receive bad news from a place of curiosity or gratitude—for the lesson, the opportunity to change, or the new doors that will open.

But then, the pandemic hit.

We looked at each other wide-eyed over Zoom with a collective HOLY SH*T!

Without judgment, we observed how high vibration beings saw the potential in this change, while low vibration beings became fearful. We understood exactly why we were being given this process. The rains had begun, and it was starting to flood. It was time to board the ark, so to speak.

We want to invite you on board the ark, too.

In this space, you are protected from the tumultuous outside world by creating energetic conditions within and around you so that you can count on your safety, security, and your needs being met, no matter what.

One thing I know for sure is that life is an inside-out job. The "out" is being shaken up, so now we must go within to find the peace and confidence that will help us to live a happy and fulfilling life and become unstoppable.

The Language of Sacred Geometry

There is a field of energy around you that can be made visible by the language of sacred geometry. Instead of a huge, wooden ship, your "ark" is energetic and geometric. For our journey to unstoppable, we will harness the energy of Metatron's Cube.

Metatron's Cube has layers and layers of meaning, from its Flower of Life structure to its containment of each of the Platonic Solids structures. Scientists love it. Mystics love it. I have come to understand that sacred geometry, specifically Metatron's Cube, can offer each of us—right now—a map to help us understand our vibrational nature. Let's allow Metatron's

Cube to guide us into a meditation practice that will initiate us into a whole new way of thriving in this new world.

The world illuminated by the news networks is only ONE version of reality, and you can shift your state of being through attention and intention to become your own Unstoppable Dream.

My Unstoppable Dream is to inspire my human family to focus on transforming this culture of fear and scarcity into one of love and abundance. I declare my Unstoppableness trusting that the dreams I dream are being given to me.

One word, one brushstroke at a time, I make the dream visible, *and* I become the dream made visible.

It's a humbling experience and a mysterious journey filled with wonderment and magic. You are here now, magnetized to these words because you, too, are meant to be unstoppable!

You want to be happy.

You want to reconnect to optimism and hope.

You want to live a purposeful life that lights you up and brings you deep joy.

You want to be a force of inspiration and change.

You have always been attracted to mystery, and you lean into what is possible.

But you have been tested. Your faith has wavered and, yet, you still sense that there is a shift happening; a matrix is unlocking that will reveal the field of pure potential you sense just on the outskirts of your imagination.

You are ready to BE the DREAM made visible.

The journey to this dream come true is an inner one. We can no longer avoid the call to, as Gandhi so eloquently said, "Be the change you want to see in the world." Whatever we desire from "out there" has to come from "within here" to be born into this reality.

We are each the creator of our own world. We have created this world, and we can create a new one. *Our logical, thinking mind will automatically resist newness because it is unknown. Resistance will persist until this dominant way of thinking perceives unity.*

Sacred geometry provides this unity and a map we can follow into the "new" we desire. Meditation provides the vehicle within which we can journey into new ways of being. Together, sacred geometry and meditation create an alchemical experience from which we emerge transformed.

This book is your map to follow on a 30-day journey within, into the unexplored landscapes of your consciousness, from which you will emerge in complete alignment with the statement, "I AM the Unstoppable Dream."

This map follows the trail laid out by the sacred geometric pattern known as Metatron's Cube. The sites we will visit along the way, in your inner realms, are energetic. They will offer you an opportunity to move into a new state of being, a vibrational landscape from which you can feel safe, secure, and loved—no matter what is going on outside you.

This journey is being guided by a consciousness that lies way outside the bounds of the physical expression named Whitney Freya. I AM the portal for this Unstoppable Dream that is your liberation from the overwhelm and worry that has become a modern epidemic.

Each chapter in this book is encoded with frequencies that will activate wisdom already present within you. You already have everything you need. Let's go within to rediscover this truth so that you can manifest all your dreams come true with grace and ease!

A Bit of the Back Story

In 1996 I opened an art center with no art training. I had never painted on a canvas when the doors opened. A year earlier, I had experienced a lightning bolt kind of ah-ha. At that moment, I was given perfect clarity that art-making and life-making were intimately connected. As if I had known it all my life, I understood that we could learn to create what we wanted to experience on the canvas, thereby learning how to create what we wanted to experience in the art that is our life.

It made perfect sense to me, even though I had never believed I could paint or draw.

So I launched myself into the extraordinary process of opening an art center. I found a 1920s-era bungalow in a run-down neighborhood in Nashville. It had been severely neglected. However, the area was slated for a significant urban renewal project, and I loved the idea of being a part of a fledgling community working together to create something new.

The house renovation was like a DIY boot camp, and I often felt a bit lost and overwhelmed by what I was leaping into. Just when I would feel the most vulnerable, magical synchronicity would happen. Fritz, the carpenter, was one such gift! This eccentric, old guy showed up on my doorstep, attracted by rumors of a renegade art center, and offered me all the colorful wood furniture he had in storage. His pieces completed the sawhorse and plywood art tables perfectly! Through the journey from crack house to soft opening, I often described the sensation of being carried along by something much bigger than me. It was like this idea that connecting art-making to life-making was a train on the move. I was being invited to hop on and steer it into existence—or not. Despite my fears of not being a trained artist or an experienced business owner, I chose to trust my instincts and hang on for the ride!

I mean, this made no sense! I didn't know how to paint and hadn't taken an art class since early high school. How could I open an art center? But I couldn't ignore the synchronicities and coincidences that were happening each day. I just knew that I wanted to be on that train!

From the very beginning of my career, when I was given my calling in life, I had to get out of my own way—all the time. I had no training or qualifications. Yet I felt this deep, deep knowing, like all the pieces of the puzzle had fallen together to guide me along a path that gave me the confidence to transcend the details and stay in alignment with the truth that was asking to be birthed through me.

I became my own Unstoppable Dream.

The Unstoppable Dream I received was the knowing that everyone is creative, that creativity can be developed, and that humans are *meant* to live life as art, not merely live it as a race or a never-ending to-do list.

This Unstoppable Dream knocked on the door of my consciousness as if to ask, "Can I come in (to this physical plane) THROUGH you?"

"Yes," I answered.

This feeling never ended. It felt like I was channeling my entire career, my soul's work. Words just flowed through me as I taught. Instantly, I would understand painting and creation elements that were popping through the ethers from who knows where... and I was lit up!

More than two decades later, if I am honest, I am still channeling my work. The golden thread is that the energy coming through me, which could easily appear as *my* passion, loves exploring all the ways we as humans can rise above our fear of living in today's tumultuous, often scary, fear-based world. This life offers us a chance to find happiness and peace and become the master of our reality. We release outdated stories and beliefs and instead embody more of our human potential as expressed through our infinite nature.

This book conveys my most recent train of thought: teaching that whatever loving, benevolent energy exists out there wants us to learn so that we can create an environment to finally shift humanity's lens from fear to love.

We are in an age of rapid change.

In your life, you have experienced incredible technological advances.

Now is the time to experience incredible advances in consciousness.

Our own internal operating systems are ready for an upgrade.

This book outlines a process that will change your life. It includes new teachings, given to me to bring out onto the paper of this book, to use as a tool for this transformational age. As old systems break down and new ones are born, you will emerge from the rubble as a thriving, creative, high vibrational being whose every need is met and whose expression is authentic and filled with pure love. This level of vibrational awareness will bathe you in peace and a sense of safety from within, regardless of what is going on in the world.

You will be illuminated to the truth of your creative power.

So, how do you stay optimistic and hopeful in these crazy times?

You become unstoppable.

Getting Started

My vision for this book is to serve you in the remembrance that you are a vibrational being who knows how to nourish and care for yourself and awaken within you a process of perceiving and creating that will liberate you from the limitations of the material world.

You may read one chapter per day for thirty days, or you may just read when you have time, allowing the ideas to sink in and become a part of your daily reality. Either way, use this book as a guiding light as you watch your world transform.

This book is designed to be experienced within your internal landscape as a guided meditation. The words, stories, and illustrations will activate you. The experience of this book will remind you that you are a vibrational being and that any feelings of being stuck, blocked, or small are ready to be transmuted into your own personal power. I encourage you to allow each day, each chapter, to sink in. Allow the ideas shared in each chapter to dance around you and inspire your musings. If the ideas challenge your rational mind, let that be okay. Let them speak to your heart.

Days 1 through 3 will introduce you to foundational elements to support your shift into unstoppableness. On Day 4, I introduce a meditation inspired by the sacred geometry Metatron's Cube that will become your "Noah's Ark," the inner vehicle from which you experience an entirely new frequency of support, flow, safety, and security in this rocky world. On Days 5 and 6, you get to know both the Flower of Life and Metatron's Cube more intimately. On Day 7, you begin the process of embodying yourself as the Unstoppable Dream, and the journey continues through Day 30.

The illustrations at the beginning of each chapter are my visual interpretation of the channeled messages in italics on the opposite page. I found this process to be extremely enlightening—and fun! I invite you to do the same in your own journal if that resonates with you. How would you illustrate that text? I can't wait to see!

And so it is.

If anything you read triggers heavy feelings within you, perhaps sparked by sadness or regret that you were not aware of this wisdom sooner, just know that everything is happening in your life in perfect timing. We learn best through contrast, from getting to know what we are not. There is no "behind," no "late," and certainly no "mistakes." Your purpose isn't to be perfect. Your purpose is to learn from the imperfect so that you might remember your inherent perfection. Trust that you are safe, guided, and all is well.

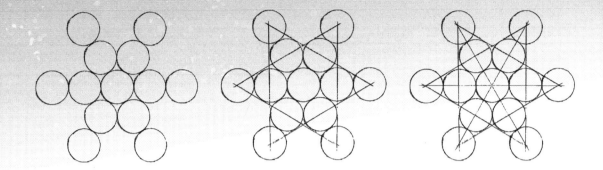

You are not here, reading these words, by accident.

You are being called into a new experience of yourself.

This journey will be an untethering of your soul.

You are liberating yourself from structures that no longer serve you
and choosing to align with the sacred geometry of life's purpose.

Be here now.

Allow the spiraling, ascending currents to carry you higher and higher.

Spread your wings. Let go of your familiar perch.

With a new sense of union, trust this new beginning.

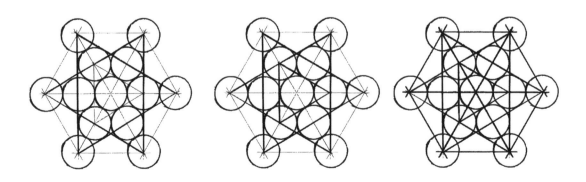

Day 1

SETTING YOUR INTENTION

Today you are invited to say YES to this journey and to set your intention for the days ahead.

I AM the Unstoppable Dream is an invitation into a state of BEing, to remember that your omniscient truth is that you are the union of spirit and matter. As such, your human consciousness is the intermediary between what "is" and what "is to be."

This state of union is WHO YOU ARE and, yet, it has become elusive, veiled by distractions, falsehoods, and fears.

The Unstoppable Dream process is an inner journey. You will remember the truth of *all* of who you are. You will receive permission to create your life with the full power of the infinite cosmos above you and the abundant eARTh below you as they meet in ecstatic union. And you will gain the confidence to move confidently in the direction of your dreams. You will cultivate a high vibration frequency that sources its power from your center—your heART.

You will shift from the frequency of DOing, which is dependent on your external world and external forces, to the frequency of BEing, which dances with your inner world and finds inspiration in the boundless landscapes of possibilities within you.

Exercise

Start by taking three deep breaths.

Then ask yourself, "What have I been DOing in my life the last couple of days?"

Then, ask yourself the question, "How have I been BEing in my life over the last couple of days?"

Do you *feel, feel, feel* the difference?

Do you receive the different truths that are the vibration of DOing or BEing?

We can *do, do, do* to the point of exhaustion. But the DOing never ends. There will always be more on the list, and we will all die with some items left unchecked.

Contemplate

Does this knowing feel heavy or light to you?

Do you sense a wellspring of truth and energy rising to the surface of your consciousness as you tap into the energy of your DOing versus your BEing?

How do you BE in your world?

What is the energy you are bathing yourself in each day?

What is the energy radiating out from you?

How do you FEEL as you move through the minutes, one by one by one?

I assure you, you *will* bring your heART's desires into your reality and live life aware of the magic and possibility available to you in each moment.

Your Unstoppable Dream simply wants you to prepare its landing pad. The entry point is made visible by BEing in alignment with the frequency of your heART, wishes, and desires, rather than your worries and fears.

You are the Unstoppable Dream when you remember that your dream is actually the Universe's dream. You are *receiving* the inspiration as the messenger, and being asked to co-create it into this physical reality *in partnership* with the infinite.

Your Unstoppable Dream does *not* need you to work harder, struggle, or strain against the physicality of life.

Your Unstoppable Dream is at the center of a mandala of energies, resources, support, and potential. It simply needs you to receive it and then, be its on-the-ground agent of action and manifestation.

You will play with the sacred symbol of Metatron's Cube to bridge the unseen with the seen. It is across this bridge that you will usher your Unstoppable Dream into your reality.

Through this process, you will receive a sacred meditative practice that will welcome you into a new awareness of how to relax into your most loving and receptive BEing. From this place, you can *trust* that when you get the call from your Unstoppable Dream, you will have everything you need to usher it into your physical experience.

How do you recognize the Unstoppable Dream?

Your Unstoppable Dream visits your consciousness as a socalled crazy idea," a familiar vision you've always had for your life or a flash of insight.

Your Unstoppable Dream may come draped in the energy of excitement, joy, or gleeful anticipation. Or, when it arrives, you feel its call in your bones; it's that moment when you FEEL, "This is why I am here." It signals to you that it wants to find a union in your heART with high vibrational states of BEing so that lower vibrational states of self-doubt, worry, or fear do not sabotage its creation.

Set your intention for this journey now. It can be small or big, simple, or complex. It can be energetic or material. Here are some ideas:

My intention is to open my heart,

My intention is to buy a home.

My intention is to raise my vibration and live from this higher perspective each day.

My intention is to start teaching and sharing my gifts with others.

My intention is to release everything that has, up until now, caused me to feel stoppable.

My intention is to fully embody my human BEing.

My intention is to open, launch, create, learn, heal, and serve.

Receive your intention now.

Welcome to your unstoppable, miracle-making Self.

And so it is.

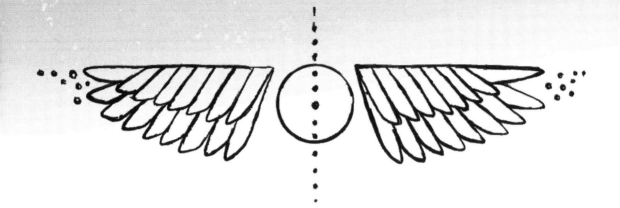

The nature of this reality is at once dense and focused, as well as light and expansive. You chose to forget your lightness of being and then to rediscover it within the shadows. Imagine a deep trench within which you can see ahead and behind; the walls are tall and straight. This is how you and others have defined who you are, what you are "good at," and what is available to you. The trench is deep so that you have not been able to see out or over its edges. It has defined your reality and your path. Today you remember that you can also raise yourself up and receive new visions of your existence and potential realities. The trench is just a small part of your story. It has grounded you and created the place from which you can rise above. It is the launch pad or the springboard into new possibilities.

SHAPESHIFTING INTO YOUR UNSTOPPABLE SELF

Today you take back more of your magic.

It is with a new awareness and attention to your state of BE-ing that you prepare yourself to shapeshift into a powerful vessel of unstoppable dream-ness!

What does it mean to shapeshift?

I had seen this word for years and been so attracted to it while also feeling that this had nothing to do with me. Shape-shifting was for werewolves and vampires, right? Shapeshift-ing happened in fairy tales and movies.

And then I got it.

Anyone can shapeshift. The werewolves and fairy tale charac-ters were just mirroring an ability we each have in a dramatic, make-believe way.

Now, you are ready to receive the process symbolized in the lands of make-believe and projected onto the silver screens.

You can shapeshift.

Don't worry; it's nothing like in a sci-fi flick. It will give you a way to navigate uncertain, shaky times, and to detach from old ways of doing and being so that you can move into your Unstoppable Self.

Think of a time when your mood switched instantly.

Maybe you got excellent news or terrible news.

Maybe an old song from your tumultuous high school years came on, and you were immediately transported back in time.

Maybe a friend called feeling upset, and you were able to conjure, at that moment, your wisest, most reassuring self to support her.

That is shapeshifting.

You have probably been doing it without awareness for a long time.

Now, we will learn to do it with awareness.

You will learn to shapeshift from your stoppable, stuck, overwhelmed, fearful self to your Unstoppable Self.

Imagine this journey is like entering a magical container that will attune and activate you to a new paradigm. You will shapeshift out of old patterns of thinking and processing and into new ways of understanding life on an energetic and quantum level. On this level, you become highly creative, creating into reality whatever is calling to you.

There are 4 steps to this process:

1. The greater the intention and resolve that you bring into this experience, the more ease you will experience in your shift.

2. You will realign your entire life's perspective from one that is predominantly focused "out" to one that is focused "in."

3. You will learn to live and create your life from energy rather than matter. Since energy precedes matter, this is the best way to manifest the changes and opportunities that you desire in your life.

4. As you immerse yourself and say YES to these first three steps, you will begin to shed the skin that is no longer comfortable and shapeshift into your new skin, more authentic and powerful than before.

Let's Practice...

I invite you now to think of something that you COULD do today. And it is something that you probably wouldn't do if you didn't have to choose it now.

It may be something you have been meaning to do or wanting to do for a long time. It could be taking time out for yourself in a bubble bath. It could be organizing a bedroom drawer. It could be calling a friend, starting to write your book, mending a hole in a sock, painting a painting, signing up for a class, having a conversation with your child.

Pick one thing that is totally accessible to you. You can easily do this thing today that you have, up until now, allowed yourself to procrastinate or avoid or deny yourself.

If you can think of nothing else, turn on the hot water and dig out the bubble bath!

Write about it below:

_____

_____

_____

_____

_____

_____

_____

_____

_____

_____

_____

_____

_____

_____

_____

_____

_____

_____

_____

_____

_____

_____

_____

_____

_____

Now, close your eyes and imagine yourself doing it.

Where are you?

What are you wearing? Or not wearing?

How do you feel?

What is around you?

Who is with you?

What is it going to feel like to complete it?

What are you going to get to do now as a result?

How are you celebrating?

Imagine yourself coming back to this page and putting a big, ol' checkmark in this box:

Done! Complete! You "shapeshifted" into the you that had this experience, that overcame inertia to be the you that experienced it. Way to go! You are a shapeshifter.

Now, instead of following up your ah-ha's and visions with all the reasons why you can't do it, you will shapeshift into the YOU that already has!

From this state of BEing, you will take new actions, one step at a time, until your dream has been made visible.

And so it is.

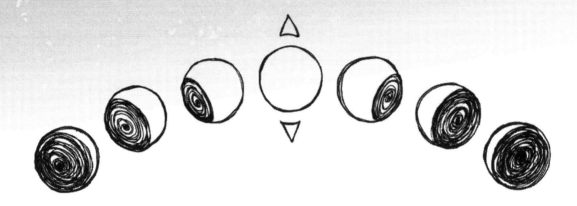

The human condition is such that it first experiences feelings of separation and scarcity.

You get to feel alone, confused, overwhelmed, and lost.

Life can feel random, scattered, and dangerous... until you remember union.

There is a pattern underlying all existence that unlocks a whole new matrix—a way of living in coherence with the wholeness of this physical experience.

It illuminates an invisible web of love and light that cradles all of existence, across space and time.

It has guided you since your conception and will lead you back to the stars.

And so it is.

Day 3

SACRED GEOMETRY

Today, the long, straight line—the deep groove of your conditioned self—remembers its sacred pattern.

You are going to cultivate a new level of energetic wellness through this meditative process. You will step into a state of BEing that is receptive, not critical; that is open, not skeptical; that is in LOVE with the vision of it, not in fear of messing it up. THEN, you will have everything you could possibly need to take brave and inspired action.

The symbol that will guide you into this state of the creative union is a mandala called Metatron's Cube. It is a powerful sacred geometric template that contains within it "The All that is All."

Mathematicians, scientists, Greek philosophers, and master artists have worked with this form and found that within its sacred geometry is union. EVERYTHING begins here. All the Platonic Solids, the building blocks of all matter, are represented in Metatron's Cube.

Often, to look ahead, it is valuable first to look back. At the core of our human journey is a tension between the rational, logical mind's desire to control and protect you from the unknown and the intuitive, creative mind's attraction to what is possible and what lies just on the other side of the "known."

During the 16th and 17th centuries, when science and factual information became the rulers of our existence, what was sacrificed was our connection to the infinite—to the possibility and potential that transcends what is "practical" or "feasible."

We closed ourselves off to a flow of wisdom and guidance that allowed us to feel connected, safe, secure, and loved on a soul level. The focus shifted to the outside world, and our inner worlds became mostly abandoned.

More recently, quantum physicists and neuroscientists have observed how the logical mind will resist all change until it perceives unity. This is because the logical mind is past- and future-oriented. It takes your experience up until now and, using that information, projects into the future to determine if the opportunity you are promoting is safe. So if you desire something new and different in your life, something you have not yet experienced, your rational mind will tell you to run the other way.

However, if your rational mind senses the presence of a unifying factor, something that bridges what you have experienced up until now with this desired future vision of yours, it will loosen its grip.

I have been given the understanding that sacred geometry provides this unity. It is the perfect union of science and the infinite, the divine design that sends innumerable galaxies spiraling through space, guiding a small seed to grow into a magnificent tree.

The meditative process offered to you on Day 5 will allow the energy of sacred geometry to loosen your logical mind's hold on your perception and guide you into an inner, vibrational state of being, ensuring that you thrive in the new world that is emerging.

You are going to shapeshift into your own walking-breathing-BEing-Metatron's Cube, a bridge between energy and matter, the union of heaven and earth, and a portal to your highest vibrational state of BEing.

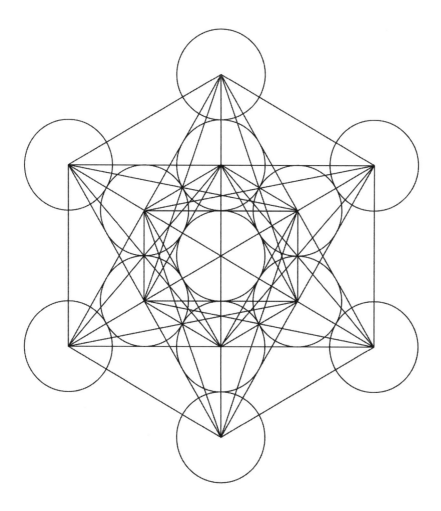

The sacred geometry of Metatron's Cube is imprinted in the cells of your being. YOU are the union of light and matter, heaven and earth. YOU are the energy of Metatron's Cube. It surrounds you energetically, and it can be expanded and activated in an infinite number of ways.

For now, simply allow it to remind you of the loving design that IS you—within and without.

Gaze at the very center point of this symbol. Imagine that you are that one point. Imagine you are that one point surrounded by all the sacred, divine energy and design. All of this energy and beauty has been hidden from you, cloaked beyond the rational mind's boundaries of perception.

Now you see.

Now you can feel and tap into the guidance and support, the reservoir of energy available to you in each moment, as symbolized in this geometric figure.

Often, as that one point in the middle, we get stuck. We feel overwhelmed and succumb to a pressure to perform that feels beyond our capacity.

However, as that one point at the center of this sacred geometry, surrounded by infinite possibility and directly connected to the mechanism of the Multiverse, you are Unstoppable!

Feel the difference?

There are multiple ways you can engage with the energy of Metatron's Cube to integrate this energy, this knowing, this level of vibration and perception. It is available to you now.

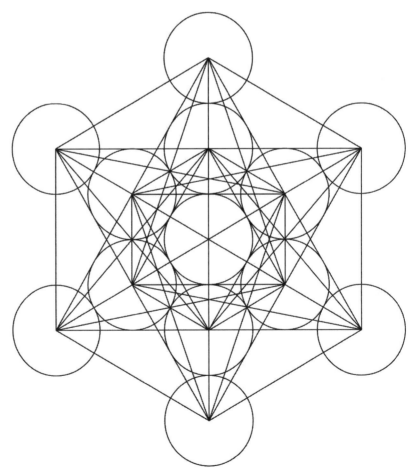

You can draw or doodle this sacred geometry symbol in your journal or paint the mandala onto any surface.

The wisdom and guidance available to us through the language of symbols is boundless. To open up more of what it offers, you can create it, look at it, and surround yourself with it. The more its energy can weave itself into the tapestry of your life, the deeper it can affect the change you desire. I wear a Seed of Life—the center part of the Flower of Life, the foundation for Metatron's Cube—as a ring as a constant reminder.

Step into a glorious journey of shape, geometry, and energy that contains the roadmap for aligning with whatever state of BEing you desire to cultivate in your life. It will disrupt your familiar, or your routine, and liberate you from patterns that can sabotage your deepest desires.

Your inner critic, your inner perfectionist, your belief in your unworthiness, and your fears of failure will dissolve into the ocean of pure potential created by the alchemy of your heART, this sacred geometry, and your high vibrational state of BEing.

Each day of the I AM the Unstoppable Dream process will include an activation. Within you, new ways of BEing and perceiving your inner world will be TURNED ON so you can see how it is intimately connected to the "all that is" and your sacred role as the space of union.

Remember, this is not about DOing. Rather, it is about nurturing and expanding your state of BEing so that YOU become THE Unstoppable Dream.

And so it is.

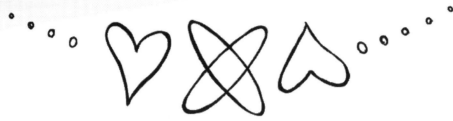

*How do I thrive in my life surrounded by such heaviness?,
you ask. You remember that you are—everything is—energy.
You remember that you and everything around you is one
vibrational being and you tend to the vibration, not matter.
Material form is temporary, but your vibration is eternal. Tend
to your vibration. Immerse your vibrational being in the energies of love, compassion, courage, alignment, gratitude, and
presence. All will be well.*

Day 4

STAYING POSITIVE IN A NEGATIVE WORLD

Today you remember that you are a vibrational being.

There is one question I am asked over and over again in my work with clients:

How do you stay positive when there is so much "wrong" with the world?

Truly, the world has a lot of scary going on; there's a lot in our lives that is justifiably stressful and worrisome.

I asked and listened, and Spirit said to me:

The human condition is inherently heavy and dense. And you are not in this life only to explore living as a human on planet Earth. If you choose, you can remember to live as a vibrational being, in a co-creative loving relationship with ALL that you are; your soul, the divine, the infinite possibility of the Universe. You get to choose.

Then, what I experienced personally in my life was a connection between my personal energy, or vibration, and my level of confidence, conviction, and optimism. I have committed to living a life guided by energy, not matter. It is a life guided by my inner world more so than the outer world. This has created the ability to be much more objective about events in the outer world and stay in my center, deeply rooted in larger, more cosmic truths. What used to happen is that what was going on outside of me had the power to knock me off my center and send me spiraling into worry, fear, and self-doubt. When things were good, I felt good. When things were bad, I felt horrible. In your center, anchored into benevolent energies that you choose to nurture in this meditation process, you are always YOU. You are not so easily shaken, and you can look objectively at the outside world and choose your BEing. You have tended your internal vibration at a big enough level that life outside has to harmonize with that vibration. Even "bad news" becomes an opportunity for learning and growing. Your "enemies" inspire compassion. You can't be shaken off your center because you have learned how to care for yourself as a vibrational BEing.

As the outer world becomes more and more contentious, worrisome, and fearful, we are being called to open up, remember, and awaken to our ability to live as high vibrational beings who GET to be embodied in physical form in this human existence. From this perspective, we are freer to experience the full spectrum of what life offers.

I AM the Unstoppable Dream is a process or a tool that we are being given to help us to thrive, to feel inspired, safe, secure, and loved no matter what is going on in the external world. In this modern society, we have been conditioned to look outside of ourselves for security and love. But, the truth is, what we are ultimately searching for can only be found within.

Since retreating to an Ashram in India or becoming a monk is not available to most of us, we are being offered initiations, or activations, through processes like this one to provide simple, accessible ways to uplevel our way of living and attune us to higher levels of vibration.

Imagine that you had an energetic light switch that has been hidden up until now. This light switch activates a light within you—a knowing, a new frequency—and wisdom. The process in this book is going to flip that switch.

Here is what I understood when my own light switch flipped on:

When I am living a life full of love, compassion, courage, alignment, gratitude, and presence, everything will be okay, no matter what. And to be living a life full of all these energies, I want to spend time and attention on cultivating these energies. When my life is defined by my commitment to generating love and compassion, everything else has to fall into place.

Now, hear me when I say this: This process does not guarantee that the economy will not crash, the virus will not mutate, or that the ozone layer will somehow repair itself. It does mean that no matter what the economy, the environment, and the politics are around me, I will be safe. I will have friends who offer me places to stay if I lose my home. I will have food if I am hungry. I will be guided when I feel lost. I am never alone.

I know this because everything is energy. The science of energy is such that like attracts like. When I am in high vibration, I trust I will attract people, circumstances, opportunities, and resources that match or exceed my vibration. It is how the Universe works.

The Unstoppable Dream Process

In the center of this symbol is YOU.
Surrounding you are your 6 Spheres of Wellness.

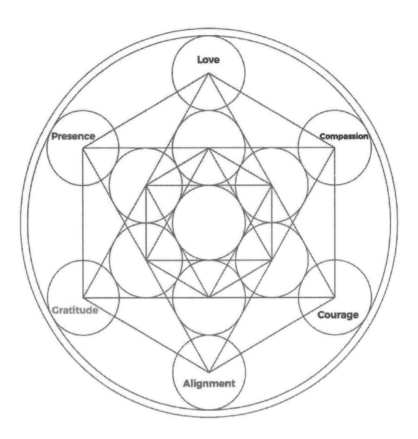

When you choose to receive this unstoppable activation, these spheres surround you at all times.

In the meditation, you will "check in" with each sphere to make sure each is full. Of course, you have the opportunity to fill up whichever sphere is feeling deficient. I imagine that each sphere looks like Glinda the Good Witch's orb in "The Wizard of Oz." Imagine having six of these luminous orbs surrounding you at all times, rotating and orbiting around you to create such a high vibrational state that you always feel guided, cared for, and loved? Let's make this your new reality, shall we?

The Unstoppable DREAM state-of-BEing becomes possible when you remember that by the time you receive the ah-ha, stroke of insight, vision, or dream that is lighting you up and getting you super excited, the dream has already made its way through layers and layers of dimensions and frequencies. YOU are the last stop before its manifestation into 3D-form. It has found you BECAUSE you have created a high vibrational state of being.

Since you are in alignment, surrounded by these six energies, and embodying your Metatron's cube, you have created a unified field. You have entered the state of union between the physical and the energetic. You are a perfect portal and YOUR dream is actually a dream being GIVEN to you because Spirit wants to experience its manifestation on Earth.

This is when you become unstoppable.

How do you achieve this state of being? You do it by cultivating the energies in the 6 Spheres of Wellness and allowing them to fill YOU, as the divine container, with their high vibration energy so that you become the Unstoppable Dream.

This meditation is intended to empower you right now to take the dream you are holding for yourself and to exponentially accelerate its manifestation into your life experience.

You may know exactly the "dream" that you are wanting to experience in your life, or you may simply be READY to receive your Unstoppable Dream, to live an Unstoppable life, or to BE the dream made visible.

Is it more important to have clarity around your dream, or to nurture within yourself the 6 Spheres of Wellness?

All I am inviting you to do now is to engage with the energies contained within these 6 Spheres and trust that as you tend to your vibrational being and your vibration rises and expands the energy around you, whatever inspiration you receive is destined to manifest because it is being *given* to you, from one high vibrational being to another.

This is the great news! The first and more important step is to align your being with the 6 Spheres of Wellness: love, compassion, courage, alignment, gratitude, and presence. Trust me, they all play very well together.

And so it is.

The earth is aware. Matter is conscious. There is not an inch on this planet that is not participating in the creation of you, your life, and the life of the collective. The Flower of Life is this consciousness. It signals the divine resonance that exists between matter and spirit. Allow the harmonies, the frequencies of this form to bring your awareness into alignment with the co-creative nature of life. As you engage with these symbols, you will be brought into greater harmony, greater resonance, with the frequency of love, the frequency of unity and the frequency of potential. Everything is a Flower of Life.

GROUNDING IN THE FLOWER OF LIFE

Today you go deeper into the activation that is sacred geometry, Metatron's Cube, and its foundational design, the Flower of Life. Connecting to these geometric designs will create a bridge. Sacred geometry is where your logical awareness and your intuitive awareness find union—where the logical mind can perceive unity. Your logical mind *wants* to perceive unity. Otherwise, it will continue to look at life through a lens of fear and attempt to block your attempts into *new*ness.

You are invited now to go within the Flower of Life Sacred Symbol. Drawing it with pencil and compass is highly recommended. (Watch this video tutorial that I created for you on YouTube at **https://youtu.be/dmjBjSenSXs**).

I have found that cultivating an understanding of how these sacred geometries are created in 2D form is extremely revealing. The process itself illuminates where you are in resonance or where there is dissonance in your energy field. Some of you will have an easy time creating or connecting with this sacred design. Some of you may want to draw it several times until you feel that "aahhhhh" that comes from the energy of creating it with all the centers lined up. It is glorious either way.

I would recommend that you give yourself at least three opportunities to draw your Flower of Life. Observe where you get frustrated and where you light up in the process. It is all symbolic and has information for you.

Read the following meditation and imagine that you are drawing the Flower of Life into being. Even in the visualization, you are receiving the activation offered to you by this sacred geometry.

Flower of Life Meditation

Engage your mind's eye, and imagine that you are sitting at a table, with pencil and compass.

Place the needle of the compass in the center of the paper, and allow your energy to be focused on that center point, as you are centering... everything about you is becoming centered.

Now, allow the tip with the pencil to rotate slowly, easily in a circular motion across the surface of your paper. Create a circle. Meditate on one circle. Receive it as a symbol of you, the individual, whole and complete, with everything you need. Breathe in this energy of wholeness.

I have everything I need.

I am complete.

I am whole.

I am loved.

I am forgiven.

I am the expression of unity.

Then look at the circle as a symbol of everything: unity, oneness, the nothingness from which everything comes.

I am we.

I am the earth.

I am the sky.

I am love.

I am possibility.

I sing through the birds.

I illuminate like the sun rays.

I am the expression of unity.

Just receive the wisdom from that circle. What does it have to say to you right now?

Pause now to journal or to receive all of the light and wisdom coming to you.

Then, when the circle has spoken, place the needle part of your compass on any point along the outline of the circle. Then, once again centered, allow the other end of the compass to trace a circle.

Now there are two circles.

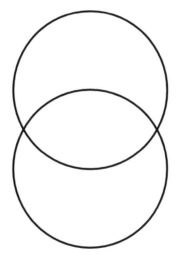

What does the center point of this second circle have to say to you? What is it symbolizing?

Imagine you, the individual, as the first circle, and you meet, or connect, with a new individual, another person, or maybe an idea, a book, a space on earth, a landscape, but there's an interaction between something other than just you. So you connect and then you become overlapped. This is also called quantum entanglement. You become a different being because of that interaction or the overlap.

Then you place the point on one of the intersections of those two circles and you draw another, and another... This image below is called the Seed of Life.

As you repeat this process and you're able to observe the sacred geometry, the Flower of Life design emerges from the Seed of Life. Notice how it could continue, and does continue, to expand in infinite time and space across all directions. Allow yourself to be the witness.

Do you notice where you lose your center? Even now as you intend to imagine this process on the canvas of your mind's eye, can you hold onto the process?

Patience.

Go back, recenter yourself. Do thoughts pull you off center? What pulls you off your center?

Allow the sacred geometry, the creation of this Flower of Life, to be a mirror.

Continue to draw or create into being the symbol that is the flower of life (in your mind's eye), and then pause.

Finish the flower of life and come back to this meditation when you can take a moment to have a conversation with the Flower of Life.

Now that you have drawn the Flower of Life, close your eyes and picture yourself as that one circle in the center, and then sense the space around you, your life, the people you know...

Notice all these other circles that have connected with you; their orbits have intertwined with yours. See your life symbolized by this flower of life pattern. Think about all the people you've met as the orbiting circles, and feel into the way you've changed their lives.

Then, they interact with other people themselves and connect and connect and connect and expand and expand...

Connect to a space in nature or imagine where you're sitting now. Become aware of your room where you're sitting as a circle, and that circle is in a particular landscape in your town.

Notice from all sides the trees, grass, flowers, the sunlight, the rain, the animals, the air, and the breath coming from all the other humans all around you.

Feel the flower of life expanding energetically through this landscape. Everything is interacting with everything. There is nothing that is not influenced by the other.

Receive the feeling of this interdependence, the interrelatedness, the oneness of everything.

Feel your own individuality dissolve into this matrix, blooming, growing, expanding, with the theme of finding your center, your wholeness, and the unity that is created when we are centered, in our power, and aware. The Flower of Life will speak to you now in exactly the way it is meant to speak to you.

Receive its wisdom as a bridge, as a portal, into remembering the unity and oneness of life. All that is, all that was, and all that ever will be.

I AM... so grateful.

You are at once, everything and nothing. You are the All That Is, that has been, can be, and will be. You are separate, that you may illuminate a unique facet of the divine, like a color on an artist's palette, and you are unified, when you choose to remember that each different color is still paint. You are a bridge, a portal, a channel through which your infinite self and the Love of Great Spirit can express and create. Now you get to remember this and to embody this truth joyfully because you have lived the illusion of separation.

Day 6

METATRON'S CUBE—
YOUR NOAH'S ARK

Today you allow this sacred symbol to heal your sense of separation.

Imagine that someone just took a picture of you with a new kind of camera. Instead of the camera capturing the image of you to which you are accustomed, it reveals an image that is typically invisible to human sight. Your friend snaps the picture and then hands you the image. This is what you see...

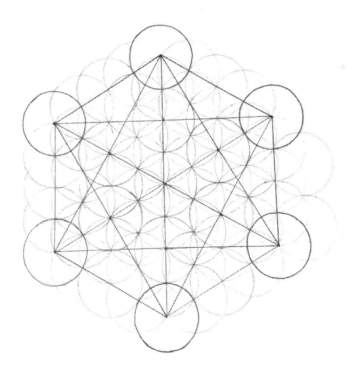

For now, simply look at this image. Connect to it on deep, unconscious levels. Allow it to speak to you.

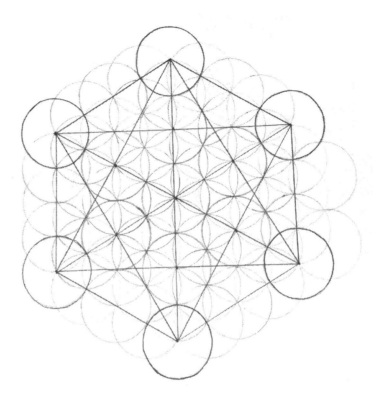

Is your attention drawn to...

- the center of the design?
- the centers of all the spheres?
- the spheres themselves, holding the edges?
- the Flower of Life pattern underneath?
- the two triangles: one pointing up and the other down?

Can you see that the triangles are pyramids?

Do you see the hexagon?

What musings are bubbling up to the surface of your awareness?

What does this symbol make you think of?

Take a moment to close your eyes and imagine yourself within this symbol. Perhaps you are sitting on the base of the pyramid that points upwards, with your hands raised, each hand touching the outer points of the base of the pyramid that points downward? Perhaps you are standing within the star, like da Vinci's man.

Feel yourself grounded and stable, supported and strong, like the upward facing pyramid. Then open up to the heavens, arms wide overhead, to receive from the stars. See yourself as the union of earth and heaven, matter and light. You are both.

Your life is characterized by the seen (the physical, material aspects of you, your dress, the color of your hair, your eyes, your home...) and the unseen (your emotions, your thoughts, ideas, dreams, desires, memories...). Up until now, most of us have allowed the tangibility and visibility of the material world to define our lives. We focus on our material being, what appears as "real."

Now, we are remembering the truth that who we really, truly are is more represented by the unseen, the energetic, vibrational aspects of who we are and what we experience energetically, emotionally, each day. You are the bridge between the seen and unseen, the energetic and the material, heaven and earth.

As soon as you recognize that you are energy first, materializing only partly into matter, the boundaries you have created to define YOU soften and blur, and you can begin to care for yourself, make decisions, and create as a vibrational being.

Look at the Flower of Life design that is the blueprint for Metatron's Cube.

Remember connecting to it as a never-ending net, or pattern, of energy and creation? This is the space of oneness.

From this field of oneness, individuals express themselves, at once unified with ALL THAT IS and also, as a unique expression of the ONE, or a fractal of the whole.

Take time now to meditate on the energy of today's activation. These are not words to be processed rationally or logically. Feel into what you have just read. Imagine each word was intended to attune you to a frequency, as a vibrational being, through which you can receive a message JUST for you.

What is the message you have received?

Write about it below:

_____

_____

_____

_____

_____

_____

_____

_____

_____

_____

_____

_____

_____

_____

_____

_____

_____

_____

_____

_____

_____

_____

To continue the dialog with this sacred symbol, you may want to draw it yourself. Check out this "How to Draw Metatron's Cube" video tutorial on my YouTube channel: **www.youtube.com/watch?v=YKrRAsWaOdM**

Feel into your sense of openness right now. Do you perceive the energy of truth rippling through your vibrational field? Do you feel the spaciousness around and within you? Allow yourself to continue to receive this energy of boundless freedom today.

These words are being offered to you now:

I AM so much more than I understood up until now.

I AM so much more than I understood up until now.

And so it is.

This meditation is alive. It is an energy who is wanting to love and inspire you. This meditation is not a test or something to tick off your list. It is an invitation into a never-ending dance, a song that never ends. It wants to weave itself into the fabric of your being, to allow you a lens through which you can see all that is possible and all that is here to support and love you. It is a reunion. It will settle with you and within you uniquely. The words, the images conjured by the words will speak to you in exactly the way that will serve your highest and greatest good. Each person who reads and receives this meditation will do so differently. Open up to how it wants to activate you. Resist attaching it to a specific moment in your history. It is like a wave that is never ending, will never, and has never, left you. Now you have the ears to hear and eyes to see. Thank you for receiving.

I AM THE UNSTOPPABLE DREAM
MEDITATION

Today you begin a meditation practice that has the potential to change everything for you. Please enjoy your first I AM the Unstoppable Dream guided meditation.

This process is very dynamic, and it is recommended to stay as open as possible to how it wants to engage with your consciousness and your energy field.

Through this meditation, you will receive the map of your journey. Within the journey are distinct experiences, facets of the whole, that can be enjoyed individually, some perhaps desiring a deeper level of communion with you than others.

In the following chapters, you will go deeper into each "Sphere of Wellness" and you will expand into your own personal understanding of what this process wants to activate within you.

Read these words to receive the energy of the meditation and then close your eyes and journey into the field of Unstoppable-ness on your own.

 **The Meditation**

Breathe deeply, inhale and exhale, three times.

Breathe into your heart and into the present moment.

Once your breath feels fluid, smooth, and deep, exhale your breath down into Mother eARTh. Imagine your breath becoming deep, luminous, energetic roots weaving down into all of Mother eARTh. Then, inhale her love and creative energy.

Breathe deeply three more times.

Then, with your next exhale, allow your breath to float gently up through the ethers, into the starlight. Feel the spaciousness. Connect to this field of pure potential. Feel the harmony as the stars and planets dance in perfect union. Feel this same spaciousness within you. Inhale this sense of possibility back down into your heart.

Feel yourself as the union of below and above.

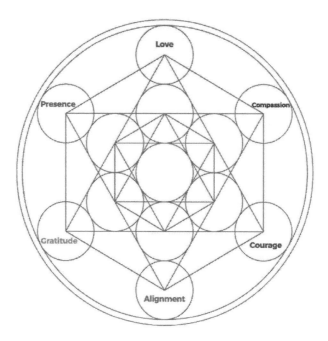

Imagine the two pyramids of Metatron's Cube coming from below and above, you in the center, receiving love and energy from Mother eARTh and Father Sky.

Breathe deeply until you can sense yourself as energy and the boundaries of your physical being dissolving into the spaciousness within and surrounding you.

Now allow your awareness to float up and to connect to the uppermost Sphere of Love.

- Feel the energy of love.
- Connect to all that you love: sunrises, a cup of tea, your children, a tree, your yoga practice, your painting practice, your friend, your partner... the flowers in your garden, the colors in your home... Simply connect to the energy of love.
- Imagine your Sphere of Love. Is it a color? Is it a light? Is it expanding? Connect to it now.

Now the Sphere of Compassion comes into your awareness.

- Feel the energy of compassion.
- Bathe yourself in the energy of compassion.
- Forgive yourself, give yourself room to try and fail.
- Self-compassion, self-compassion, self-compassion.
- Feel compassion for those who are hurting.
- Feel compassion for those who are in need.
- Send compassion to warring parts of the planet.
- Send compassion to the children who are alone.
- Feel, be, bathe yourself in compassion.

The Sphere of Courage now comes into focus.

- Breathe in the energy of courage.
- When have you felt courageous? Feel it again.
- Who do you consider courageous?
- Imagine yourself being courageous in new ways. You are already there. Choose this energy.

Imagine the Sphere of Courage filling with light, with energy, with color... Imagine it expanding, circling around you and bathing you in courage.

The Sphere of Alignment.

- Breathe this energy in from the bottoms of your feet, all the way up and through the crown of your head.
- Feel yourself strong and straight, like a great oak tree.

- Imagine anything that is not in alignment falling away effortlessly like leaves from a tree in fall.
- Imagine yourself living in alignment, in your truth, authentically, expressing yourself honestly and completely.
- I AM in alignment.
- I honor all that feels in alignment with my truth, my individuality.
- FEEL alignment.

The Sphere of Gratitude.

Allow the list of all for which you are grateful to wash over you, like you are sitting under a luminous waterfall of gratitude.

- I am grateful for...
- I am grateful for...

Now, the Sphere of Presence appears to bless you.
- Breathe into the present moment
- All that you know is right now.
- Now.
- Now.
- The past melts away.
- The future dissolves into the present.
- You are here now.
- In the present moment you are pure energy and possibility.
- You are infinite.
- You are released from any past experiences and any future worries.
- Presence.

Feel these energies swirling, spinning, orbiting around you, creating a luminous web of light, color and energy. This is your Noah's Ark. This is your protection, your security. Energy is energy. Like attracts like. You are a magnet for all that is in harmony with this vibrational field surrounding you.

Say aloud:

"I have so much more available to me than I have perceived up until now."

"I have so much more available to me than I have perceived up until now."

You are Unstoppable.

And so it is.

Your life's purpose is to rediscover that love is the only eternal truth. Every single thing, experience, person, and challenge on this planet is here to love you. Nothing can exist outside of love. Love dances with the positive and the negative in life. It takes away to create space for newness and it adds into your life experience that which will, ultimately, guide you back to your heart. Love is from which you came and to which you will return.

Day 8

THE 1ST SPHERE OF WELLNESS—**LOVE**

Today you get to surround yourself with your Sphere of Love.

What are all the things you love?

Right NOW what comes to mind?

Can your mantra today be, "What else do I love?"

Energy does not have hierarchy. There is not better or worse when it comes to energy—love energy is love energy. Loving fluffy pancakes in the moment is just as "good" as loving a sunset, a child's laugh, or your beloved.

The more you tune in to all the ways you are ABLE to LOVE in each moment, the higher your vibration will go. You can look for all the ways you get to love through life, people, places, and things, knowing that the more you love, the more love will find you.

The more you be, create, share, radiate...love... the more in alignment you will become with your UNSTOPPABLE-ness.

Enjoy the following meditation and allow it to ripple through your awareness for the rest of the day, like waves lapping up onto the shore. Integrate the energy and wisdom coming to you in this meditation. Flow with this current. Get curious about all the ways life can BE and FEEL different when you are always on the lookout for more ways to love.

To receive this meditation, I hiked into the wilderness near my home. I source much of my personal energy, the teachings that come through me, and my vibrational wellness from Mother eARTh. I desired to channel this meditation in a state of union with eARTh and heaven.

I found a magical tree, a huge ponderosa pine, and sat under it. As soon as the meditation began to speak through me, there was a large CRACK! POP! Someone on the other side of the wilderness boundary was having target practice. My first reaction was, "Dang! That just ruined this meditation."

Just as quickly as the disturbing sound shattered my "flow," I received the guidance, "Everything is here to support you. How is this here to support you?" In that moment, I was bathed in the understanding that I was just given a symbol of the perfect contrast between living exclusively as a physical being and living as a vibrational being. One is fleeting while the other is expansive. Without much of a pause, the meditation continued.

As much as the sound of the sharp explosion unsettled me, it also provided me with the perfect understanding of what we can choose through this process.

I share this meditation with you now—with so much love:

Love Sphere Meditation

In this meditation, we are going to fill up our first Sphere of Wellness with the energy of love.

Take three DEEEEEEEEEPPP breaths.

In...

Out...

In...

Out...

In...

Out...

Allow your sense of your edge to soften. Feel the air around you, the temperature of the air. Connect to the sounds, sensing the energy buzzing all around and within you. And breathe into your heart. Allow your heart to radiate the feeling of love.

Feel into that love. Close your eyes, and imagine sitting under a big, beautiful tree warmed by the sunlight, birds chirping, feeling connected, feeling so supported, one with the energies around you. POP! CRACK! That sound is quick and fleeting. It's a crack in the moment, a pop.

And then back to nature.

So, living life as an ordinary human who's not tapped into the extraordinariness of this life—it's like someone who only hears the momentary, shocking BOOM!—who thinks that quick crack pop in the ethers is it.

You can see how scary that would be.

That quick, sharp, loud pop, the energy, anxiety, the star-tled-ness..,

Am I safe? Am I secure? What's going on?

This is the frequency that we tap into when we forget the love that is all around us, wanting to be created through us, as the infinite nature of who we are and what we have available to us.

The invitation before you now is to live rooted, grounded in the massiveness of the abundance and the manifesting creative power of Mother Earth while also reaching to the sky in the light, charging in every moment from the infinite Universe. Infinite Potential, ideas, inspiration, and wisdom lie just on the other side of this next thought for you. Imagine you could reach out your hand into the nothingness and pull in whatever it is you need right now.

You get to choose.

So, breathe into your heart and imagine yourself leaning against this big ponderosa pine tree, and send your roots down, down, down into the ground.

Down...

Down...

Down...

Feel how you are provided everything you need to stay healthy and powerful, to be a vehicle through which the Infinite can create your physical body as the portal, nurtured by Mother Earth.

Sink your roots down, down, down.

And then, as you feel yourself nurtured and you breathe in all the resources, all the support from Mother Earth, also feel yourself reaching up from your trunk, from your heart, up, up, up through the crown of your head.

Up...

Up...

Up...

A big strong tree trunk reaching up, up, up, stories and stories, tens of feet, 30, 40, 50 feet into the sky with an uncountable number of needles, of fingers, of arms outstretched to the light, receiving all the guidance, all the wisdom, all the insight, all the awareness you need.

Breathe that energy into your heart, and ask for yourself, this vehicle, to be filled with the sensation, the energy, the feeling of love.

Allow all the things that you love to come into your awareness.

Dark chocolate,

sunrises,

a child's laugh,

the color orange...

The scent of pine needles being heated in the sun.

Fluffy pancakes,

your favorite slippers,

putting your head down at night,

cozying up in your comfy bed,

your best friend,

your pet,

playing Monopoly.

Building a fire in your house.

That moment when you dive into the water in the lake or the pool.

Floating down a river,

taking a hike,

sipping tea with lemon and honey,

cooking an artichoke,

a good hair day,

a good hug,

the color magenta,

that feeling that you get when you get a new idea, a stroke of insight, an aha.

The way you light up when you see that special someone.

Finding the perfect pair of jeans that fits you like a glove.

Warm socks,

a beach,

a perfectly ripe peach,

a summer night.

The stars when they're so clear,

when you remember a constellation.

Sharing something meaningful with a good friend,

being there when your good friend needs you.

That feeling in meditation when you drop in,

when the painting reaches that point that inspires an, "Ooh, I love it."

All the things you love, all the ways love comes through you.

You can now love the way life provides you with contrast, opportunities that ultimately deepen and strengthen your love.

I love that I'm remembering.

I love that I'm doing the work.

I love the teachers that appear when I am ready.

I love all the ways I can offer and teach others.

I love life because of the contrasts.

I love how I'm able to feel free and liberated because I've also felt trapped.

I love the way I'm able to express myself because I also know what it's like to hold back and to edit my thoughts and my words.

I love sunrise, because I also love the dark night.

I love the moments when I feel illumination and positivity.

And I can love and appreciate that I love those things because I've also felt stuck and uninspired and hopeless.

I AM love made visible.

I AM love in my life.

I receive all the ways that this life is here to love me, and all the ways I can radiate love out into this life.

Love, loving, being love is part of my purpose in this life.

I AM love.

I AM Unstoppable.

And so it is.

Watch the video in which I receive this meditation here:
https://vimeo.com/393556346/3139e6eea7

The audio version is available here:
http://bit.ly/lovespheremeditation

You came here to learn, to grow. You came here to express yourself in ways you have never expressed yourself before. You chose the "canvas" that is being human on planet eARTh right NOW because it contrasts your infinite state of being. You came here to create coherence between failing and succeeding, between love and hate, between the positive and the negative, between right and wrong. Because you are now remembering that everything is here to love you, and that you are a vibrational being, not just a physical being, you are seeing clearly how you have been your own worst obstacle. You have criticized and berated yourself. You have demanded perfection in a field created to flow with imperfection. Can you see now how your physical self deserves your own compassion? Can you promise today to get better and better at cheering yourself on, at picking yourself up when you fall, with words of kindness and promises of unconditional support? Can you be grace and forgiveness for yourself in new ways starting now?

Day 9

THE 2ND SPHERE OF WELLNESS—COMPASSION

Today you will open up to all the new ways you can be compassionate... with yourself.

How is compassion different from love?

You can LOVE yourself, love the way you sing, dance, act as the mediator, look on the bright side of things, and laugh with your full belly at your friends' jokes.

You can be COMPASSIONATE with yourself...

> ...when you try something new and you don't live up to your own expectations.

> ...when you lose your temper or say something hurtful to another.

> ...when you don't do that thing every day like you intended.

> ...when you get "behind."

> ...when you jump the gun and make assumptions that cause conflict.

> ...when you doubt your abilities or shrink from a new opportunity.

...when your family makes you mad.

...when you allow fear to keep you from stretching into new experiences.

...when you make a mistake.

What are all the ways you can be the encouraging voice for yourself that you want to hear from another?

What are all the ways you can...

...forgive yourself?

...mother yourself the way you wish you were mothered?

...father yourself the way you wish you were fathered?

...listen to yourself the way you wish you were listened to?

To fill up your Sphere of Compassion, first practice witnessing yourself as a parent might witness a young child.

Catch yourself doing things right:

"Wow, I am really great at putting bread in the toaster! And then I rock the butter step!"

Encourage yourself when something doesn't work out the way you expected:

"Way to give it a go, Self!"

Accept your humanness:

"Look at my human self losing my SH%T in the rush hour traffic!"

And ALWAYS let yourself know that you believe in YOU.

Check in now with your own Sphere of Compassion. Is it full? Halfway full? Running on empty?

Now, think back to a time recently when you were self-critical. Or maybe your inner perfectionist demanded better and you felt like you failed. Perhaps you said something "wrong" or fell back into an old routine when you had tried so hard to create a new habit.

Do you have it?

Now, say to yourself...

I am SO worthy.

I will keep trying.

I learn more and more every day.

I now have more clarity around what I do want.

I have everything I need.

It is okay to try and to fall short.

It is perfect to forgive my 'imperfections.'

I am trying.

There will be another chance.

I am loved.

And so it is.

Notice now the feeling of being in your known. It feels familiar. You feel safe here. You may feel like an expert here or an authority on this known landscape of your life. You have the routine down. You do it well. There is security here. And yet.. life is calling you into something new. You have seen something or heard something that has generated an involuntary "Ooooh!" from within your heart.

"I want that. I want to do that. I want to be like that. I want to experience that. That looks fun. That would be amazing..."

Then, what happens? Some of you follow that energy all the way to the realization of the vision and desire. You lean into new territory. You risk making a mistake. You might even "fail" the first couple of times. You persist. And then, when you least expect it, you are on the other side of that newness. The leap has come and gone and you are standing solidly on new ground. You were courageous. You talked yourself through that threshold when you stepped over from the known into the unknown. You believed in yourself enough to trust that you had what it takes to learn and embody this newness.

Or maybe you didn't. Instead of following the path that was illuminated by the spark that got lit up inside of you, perhaps you held back. You allowed the fear of what might happen, what mistakes might be made, what rejection, disappointment, or failure might come to stop your forward movement into that newness.

Can you bathe yourself in self-compassion now? Can you forgive your distrust in your ability to leap and land safely? Do this now. There is no judgment. There is learning along both paths, and wisdom gained. Feel the spaciousness you truly have within your human experience.

Day 10

THE 3RD SPHERE O₁
WELLNESS—**COURAGE**

Today you create space for your courageous self.

After reading the transmission on the opposite page, ask yourself:

Do I want to align with the part of me that is COURAGE made visible?

If the answer is yes, read on.

One of the things we humans love to do is to label or categorize life.

I am this... I am not that.... I can... I can't...

We create structures and boundaries that we intend to use to create feelings of safety and love. Or are you sacrificing the freedom and expansiveness that is available to you by trying to protect yourself from failure, from making a mistake or from being rejected?

Today let's try on a new state of objectivity, one that will enable you to observe the nature of your vibrational being-ness.

Where is your vibrational self being fenced in and where are you allowed to roam?

you are not acting from a place of courage, what are you afraid that you might experience?

Are you afraid of...

- Making a mistake?
- Being wrong?
- Not being good enough?
- Being rejected?
- Being seen?
- Messing it up?
- Losing something material in your life such as your home, or your ability to spend money on travel or new clothes?

Again, employ objectivity. Be your own witness.

Once you go one layer under your fear by asking these questions, you will probably realize you truly have nothing to fear. The fear doesn't stand up when you challenge it even a little bit.

To fill up your Sphere of Courage, we first courageously observe its opposite.

Where are you holding back?

Where are you being meek?

Where are you playing small?

Be with this. Allow any judgment or feelings of unworthiness to ripple through your vibrational being. Allow the truth to ripple out to where you can see it. Send it love. Bathe it in self-compassion. You cannot truly fill yourself with the energy of courage until you have unconditionally felt and accepted its shadow.

As a vibrational being, as the Unstoppable Dream, you accept everything in your life, you receive unconditionally, and then you choose. You redirect your focus. You send your awareness, newly informed by time spent in these shadowy spaces, towards that which you want to illuminate.

Do you feel the space that is being created now? Even if your experience up until now has been less than ideal, with the energy of courage, it does not mean that same experience has to be a part of your now, or your future.

Let's create space for courage to dance in your vibrational space.

Where are you being called into newness? Allow this new awareness of where you have been in fear to illuminate where you want to leap from a place of love and trust.

What are all the ways you can fill up your Sphere of Courage? There are little ways and big ways. Anything that activates the vibration of courage within your vibrational being IS courage. Energy is energy. Answer the following questionsl:

With my courageous self I want to:

_____

_____

_____

_____

_____

_____

_____

_____

_____

_____

_____

_____

_____

I am full of courage so that now I can:

_____

_____

_____

_____

_____

_____

_____

_____

_____

_____

_____

_____

_____

_____

I act courageously by:

_____

_____

_____

_____

_____

_____

_____

_____

_____

_____

_____

_____

_____

_____

_____

_____

_____

_____

_____

_____

_____

You can get courageous at work today, when you talk with your family, your child, your spouse or lover. You can be courageous as you cook, as you exercise, as you reach out to an old friend. You can courageously express yourself in your journal, in a letter to your mother, or as you paint.

Today you create space for courage to dance with you. Turn up the music and go for it!

I know how it feels to be courageous.

I choose to follow the wisdom of my heart.

I embrace that change includes stepping into the unknown.

The unknown is where I get to experience change.

I am cultivating all the courage I need to follow my highest path.

And so it is.

Your life is not a journey from A to B. It is a dance. Swirling around you at any moment are supporting energies, contrasting energies, and opportunities to expand. There is an invisible matrix of support and guidance that becomes visible when you loosen your grip on what you think and open up to receive how you feel.

Day 11

LOVE, COURAGE, & GRATITUDE

Today you tap into the energies dancing all around you!

There is a beautiful connection between the Spheres of Wellness that share space on the same triangle in our Metatron's Cube.

There is an invitation to receive how they want to support and complement one another. They illuminate for the other new ways to grow and expand each energy around you.

Look at these three Spheres: Love, Courage, Gratitude.

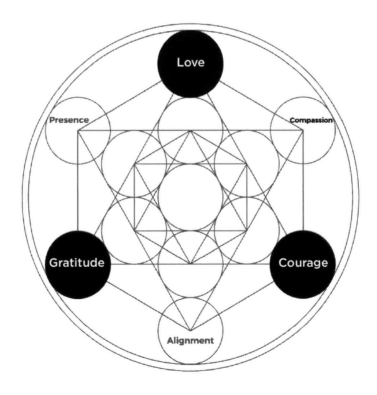

How do they want to dance in your awareness?

Where do you want more courage to love bigger?

How can love support you in the areas of your life that are calling for courage?

Can focusing on gratitude expand the love and courage that is available to you?

As we move around and through your Unstoppable Dream process, allow the expansive, starlight, cyclical nature of this journey to settle into your heart. It is not a "first, this, then, that..." kind of journey. It is everything and nothing at once. It is the light and the dark swirling together. It is the support from above and below and around you, meeting you where you are and asking always for you to open more... to trust more...

With more courage, what else might you love in your life?

With more gratitude, where else might you discover reservoirs of courage?

What is it that you love that could be expanded with your gratitude?

What are the flip sides of each?

How does hating something cultivate fear?

How does fear distract you from focusing on all for which you are grateful?

How does taking something or someone that you love for granted, the absence of gratitude, cause your love sphere to also be depleted?

The forest fire clears way for new growth.

The darkness allows the starlight to exist.

The downpours nourish new growth.

The failures create greater pools of resolution to fuel our ultimate feelings of accomplishment.

When you have felt trapped, has that not led to your liberation?

Read these words and then close your eyes to feel the energy:

You are a holograph. You are the everything contained within the one thing. You have oceans, teaming with life and energy within you. You are a universe of possibility, your own solar system, with energies spinning and cycling in perfect harmony. You contain within you the memories and the dreams of all of humanity. You exist in the now, the past and the future. You have the wisdom of the sages and saints waiting at the shoreline of your awareness. And you have the innocence of a child, the seed of the fruit tree, waiting to burst forth, to grow and to feed the world. You are the drop of water just before it dives into the surface of the still pond and you are the cyclone of thoughts and musings that tear through old realities and clear the way for new ways of expression. You are light made visible and matter longing to dissolve into the ethers. You are the layers of life and experience and emotion that have formed deep canyons and the highest mountain peaks. You are you. You are him. You are her. You are us. We are you. Namaste.

And so it is.

You've been conditioned to pay more attention to what other people think of you than what you think of you. You have been rewarded for making others happy, for living up to their expectations and this has created dissonance within and around you. You are a unique, individual expression of the Infinite. As that unique, individual expression you are meant to be, to live and to create as YOU desire. The Infinite does not create a unique individual to express itself like something else. You are meant to be you, completely, unapologetically, shamelessly, fearlessly YOU. This journey is bringing you within and guiding you into your own heart, your own desires, wishes and dreams, your beliefs and stories. It is there that you find alignment and only from this space of alignment can you fulfill your purpose, the sign of which is pure joy.

Day 12

THE 4TH SPHERE OF WELLNESS—**ALIGNMENT**

Today you begin to release all that is no longer in alignment.

I love that our Sphere of Alignment falls directly under the Sphere of Love, as it passes through the center, which is YOU; YOU as the Unstoppable Dream! Let's nurture this Sphere of Alignment with the following 4 steps.

Step 1: Let go of feeling responsible for others

We often hold on to a job, a relationship, a pattern of behavior, an expectation, or a story because we are afraid that if we let go we will hurt, disappoint, or even anger others.

You are not responsible for anyone else's happiness or well-being (save your children until they reach an independent age— even then, you can't live their life for them) simply because of the truth that you can't make anyone else be happy or well if they are making choices that are not in alignment with happiness or wellness. Only they can do that for themselves.

You are not responsible, nor is it possible, to BE for someone else the way you would wish for them to BE. Can you begin to let go of this feeling of responsibility now? Can you intend, each day from now on, to ask yourself what serves YOUR highest and greatest good?

"I don't want to be selfish" is a false belief—a lie—that has been told to you. When all people begin to take care of themselves and their mental, emotional, spiritual, and physical energy, with no blame and no victims, we will be living Heaven on eARTh.

You are hereby given permission to be SELF-centered, to go within to create the life you were born to live. No one else can do that for you.

Now, we are better prepared to fill up our Sphere of Alignment.

Step 2: Create as many experiences as possible that make you happy

What lights you up from the inside out? Where do you want to dissolve into the present moment, never to return? Do more of that. Only when you tune into and experience these elevated emotions can you allow them to guide you into alignment. If you do not know joy (have you experienced that energy lately?) you can hardly be a healthy, vibrant vibrational being.

It is not possible to follow the energy of apathy, obligation, boredom, or frustration into alignment.

Joy was given to you to signal your life's purpose, and encourage you to continue along the path that inspires joy within you. It's a signal you receive in your vibrational field, when you are engaged in a way that is resonant with your highest good.

The message you are being offered in moments of joy is, "Yes! More of this, please!"

The better it feels, the more time you will spend with this energy. The more time you spend in this energy, the higher vibration you will reach. The higher vibration you reach, the more you can receive your highest guidance and be the portal through which the Infinite can create. Then you become "Our" Unstoppable Dream!

This does not mean you are experiencing joy 24/7. It means you are regularly engaged with things, people, jobs, and places that make you happy and joyful!

Here's another clue: What have you ALWAYS done, since you were a kid, that has made you happy?

I was talking with a client about her plans to speak and teach more online and in person. She made an exclamation, "I just gotta teach!" Then, she went on to share how as a child, she would line up stuffed animals, even jars of nail polish, in orderly student-like rows. Then, she would take attendance. The stuffed animals would raise a hand, "Here!" and the nail polish jars would stamp out their answer, as they had no hands to raise! She IS, was sent here, chose to be... a TEACHER.

I remember hearing that we are our most authentic selves at age eight. At age eight, among other things, I had an art center in my basement. The space under the stairs was painted all red and the words ART CENTER were stenciled in white on the wall. I was teaching creativity even then.

What have you always LOVED to do? And what are all the ways you can do more of that now? Climbing trees, swimming, painting, exploring, acting, building, taking things apart? This isn't about your career and earning income, although it can lead to that.

Being in alignment and nurturing this Sphere of Wellness is about being a person regularly engaged in joyful activity so that you glow, your energy lights up the grocery store line, and your friends lean in to learn "what you've been doing." Simply living at a higher vibration will attract to you more and more high vibration. From this space, you become Unstoppable.

This leads to the third step in achieving consistent alignment.

Step 3: Make your inner child super happy

In many traditions there is an understanding of the three selves: the higher self, the child self, and the adult self. These three selves have a line of communication. The higher self can communicate with the child self and the child self with the adult self. The adult self can ONLY reach the higher self via the child self. This is why there is so much guidance encouraging us to nurture our inner child.

Want to find your purpose? Play. Have fun. Make yourself happy.

In those moments, you will experience alignment. The more present you become, the more you will feel in flow. In the present moment, you do not have the father you are trying to impress or the story from your elementary school teacher repeating in your mind. You are only you.

Step 4: Receive a symbol that FEELS like alignment to you

What is an image that communicates to you the energy of alignment, and also misalignment, and what it feels like for you?

For example, imagine one of those long, steep water slides, with all the different sections of tubing that create the twists and turns on your way from the top to the pool at the bottom. Now, imagine those tubes, those connections, being out of alignment. Ouch!

Or maybe you connect with trying to shine a light down a long, straight tunnel or a super curvy one. You won't be able to see much with all those zigs and zags, right? Or maybe it is even more un-romantic like imagining your house's plumbing. That is somewhere you want lots of flow! Can you feel the energy of alignment now? Guide yourself into that feeling.

Now, here's the work: Everything you do, say, think, and create wants to be in alignment.

Is your daily conversation around the dinner table, or the water cooler, in alignment with what you desire to experience more of in your life?

Do your thoughts inspire your dreams or shoot holes in them?

Are the words that exit your mouth supportive of what you would want to expand in your life or do they nurture feelings of doubt, dissatisfaction, struggle...?

Your UNSTOPPABLE Self speaks, thinks, and creates in perfect alignment.

Your body and your breath can help to guide you into deeper alignment. Imagine your breath is the water from the waterslide or the beam of light shining into the tunnel. Inhale and fill up with the light.

Inhale the light through the crown of your head and imagine the light shining through your head, down your throat, to your heart, into your solar plexus, your belly and your seat.

If you are familiar with the chakras, you are inhaling through the crown chakra, into the 6th chakra, your third eye, down the 5th chakra, the throat chakra, into the 4th chakra, your heart, your 3rd chakra, solar plexus, your 2nd chakra, belly, and finally, your 1st, or root, chakra.

Do you feel alignment or does your breath, the light, the energy, get stuck somewhere?

Allow your exhale to travel back up from your root to your crown and then, repeat. The light is traveling in a smooth line up and down your body.

Breathe like this, deeply and slowly, until you feel clear, and the energy within you is flowing and in alignment. You are nurturing this feeling of alignment, which will make it obvious to you when an energy enters your vibrational space that is not in alignment. This is the great news. Instead of worrying about what you need to let go of to get into alignment, you can spend time connecting to the feeling of alignment, doing more of what is in alignment with THAT feeling! You don't have to run out and quit the job or "break up" with the friend or lover, simply spend more time doing what you love. You may be surprised how what happens next, with so much ease, adds to your Sphere of Alignment.

You now get to open up to ALL the things you do, thoughts you think, activities, experiences, relationships... that ARE in alignment with your Unstoppable YOU! Focus on these energies in your life and allow those that are not in alignment to detach and drift softly into the nothingness.

And so it is.

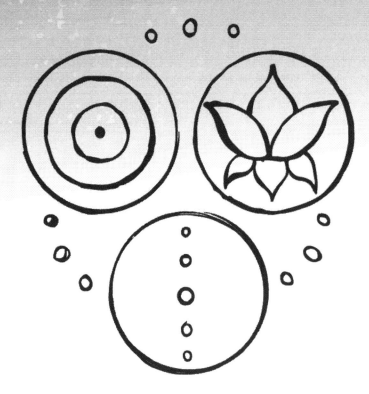

Feel yourself sitting safely and securely on Mother eARTh. Feel yourself supported by the ground underneath you, the co-creative energies swirling all around and within you that are in harmony with the eARTh elements. You are in your upright pyramid, grounded and pointing towards the heavens. Love, Courage, and Gratitude are your touchstones here. Now reach your awareness up to receive the descending pyramid of energy from the sky above. This pyramid is energetically aligned with the energy of the infinite, of pure, boundless possibility, with the energies that will empower you to create into physical reality that which is desiring to physicalize or become part of our eARThly experience: compassion, alignment and presence. It is the truth of the infinite potential combined with the energies to help you to choose, to receive, and to focus. These energies are gifts from the stars to help you to be and feel Unstoppable.

COMPASSION, ALIGNMENT, & PRESENCE

Today you explore a trifecta of energies that allow you to tap into your infinite possibility.

In any creative process or experience there are divergent energies at play. In order for a seed to grow (up), it must first be buried (down). In order for it to be able to receive light (sun), it has to absorb essential energies in the dark (soil).

Before you can jump up, you first will bend down.

If you are open, open, open... without taking the next step of choosing, you will never create the unknown into the known, the unseen into the seen.

So, maybe...

Compassion is sent to help you stay in action during the creative process of your Unstoppable Dream, otherwise the inevitable setbacks and mis-steps might conjure up too much critical energy.

Alignment is sent to create a narrower opening through which the dream can be born. If everything was in alignment how could you possibly co-create everything? There has to be some dissonance so that you can recognize alignment.

And it is only in the present moment, liberated from your past experiences and doubt about the future, that you can open fully to choose and to create.

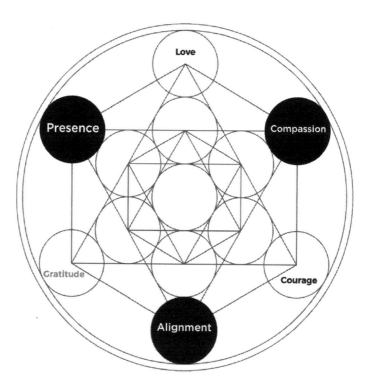

Can the present moment help you see a situation or a person through the lens of compassion, rather than transferring onto it or them an old story or past memory?

You are here to create a life, life experiences, opportunities and relationships that are, at their foundation, energies that we would want to ripple through time, over and over, loving everything that it touches. Your creations are rooted in compassion, the desire to serve, in alignment with your heart, and fueled in the present moment.

Close your eyes now.

Feel yourself sitting comfortably, supported in your upward pointed pyramid, surrounded by love, courage and gratitude. Now, receive the pyramid from above, filling you up from above with compassion, alignment and presence.

Compassion.

Alignment.

Presence.

Are you served by presence to let go of past patterns of being self-critical, or blaming others, and generate compassion for yourself, someone else, or a situation?

Does compassion free you to choose a dream that is in alignment with your highest vibrational self because you no longer fear making mistakes or failing?

What synergy are you shown now between the energies of compassion, alignment and presence?

Bring your musings into this physical reality by writing them down below:

_____

_____

_____

_____

_____

_____

_____

_____

_____

_____

_____

_____

_____

_____

_____

_____

_____

_____

_____

_____

_____

_____

_____

_____

_____

_____

_____

_____

_____

_____

_____

_____

_____

_____

_____

_____

_____

_____

_____

_____

_____

_____

_____

_____

_____

You are a compassionate being, living in alignment, present to all that is possible.

And so it is.

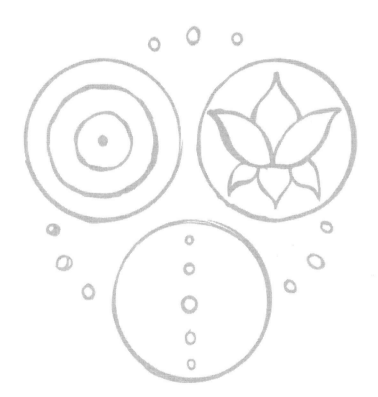

You forgot to teach each other that everything is alive, everything has consciousness. You were taught to say "please" and "thank you" to your parents, your teachers, but not to the earth and sky. Your modern culture chose not to acknowledge the roles played by the natural world, the animals, the elements, and the unseen energies that make your life possible. They desire your "please" and "thank you" as well. When you express gratitude, you are not merely "thanking" the object of your gratitude, you are acknowledging the value it holds in your life. You are in a state of receiving when you express gratitude, not forcing or controlling. This receptive state allows you to open up to new ways of receiving even more. Without the energy of gratitude, you are simply taking. You are minimizing the role of the world outside of you, and creating for yourself an island where only you matter. You do this without awareness. Today you begin your return journey into the fold of creation, humbly approaching this truth with gratitude.

THE 5TH SPHERE OF WELLNESS—
GRATITUDE

Today you bathe yourself in gratitude.

In the book, *Notes and Methods,* Hilma af Klint shares a message that she and four other women, known as *The Five,* received from the "masters" and documented in their detailed notes from one of their sessions.

They are told that there is a "secret growing" that surrounds every living element on the planet, supporting, nurturing, and providing for each animal, rock, stream, and flower. What spoke most vividly to me was how the "masters" described this unseen presence surrounding each flower, guiding it from seed to germination to the unfurling of each leaf and the bloom of each flower.

The Five are reassured that this same energy surrounds each person.

> *"When you do not see an outer result, this must not discourage you...for just as invisible hands help and tend every plant on this green Earth, so every budding sprout of goodness is tended and shaped and protected by invisible powers..."*

> —Hilma af Klint, *Notes and Methods*, 2018, Christine Burgin, University of Chicago Press

In this channeling, you are encouraged to trust that even if you feel like all of your efforts up until now have been futile or fruitless, this unseen presence is working and you will eventually witness the fruition of your desires.

Back to your breath...

You can connect to this unseen presence right now through the element of air, your breath. Is it not an unseen presence, a presence without which you would cease to exist in this human form? Bring your awareness to your breath now. Inhale deeply, 1-2-3, pause at the end of your inhale. Then, exhale, 1-2-3. Pause. Repeat.

As an example, connect to the idea of your breath right now.

Your breath... but is it?

What was it, whose was it before it became your breath? It was the air, the wind, the gentle breeze...

It was transformed into oxygen by the flora outside your window. Before that transformation it was also the wind and, perhaps, the exhale of your neighbor, or your dog or cat.

Imagine you can visually witness your exhale for the next 48 hours, as it leaves your lips and proceeds on its journey and repeated transformations. Could this be what the unseen presence looks like as captured by Hilma af Klint?

Now, express gratitude for your breath. Once you do, you realize that you can't stop there. You want to give thanks to the air and the wind.

Now, send your gratitude to the trees and all the flora around your home, in your town, around the planet. All of it has been a co-creator of just one of your breaths.

You can surround yourself with gratitude... to your breath...

Feel into HOW MUCH there is to be grateful for right now. How about the water in your glass? Send gratitude to the mechanics that deliver it so conveniently to the tip of your faucet. Send gratitude to all the forces and beings that purify this glass of water for you. Now, thank the rain, the rivers and streams, lakes and oceans. Send gratitude to your exact watershed, the source of your water. Imagine all the times just one water droplet has been transformed from ether to cloud, to rain, to snow, to river, to stream, to ocean and back to the ethers.

Gratitude.

For today, connect to the elements of nature, the energies that support the growth and cycles, the people that grow your food, that transport it, and make it available to you. Receive the gift of light and warmth from the sun. Receive the shade from the tree, the beauty from the lake, the mountain, the river.

Choose to cultivate this energy of gratitude from the most routine elements of your day. Thank the earth for supporting the foundation of your home, the birds for their song, the sun for nourishing the trees and plants all around you.

Fill up your sphere of gratitude by choosing to receive the gifts of the natural world that operate in such perfect balance, in spite of our neglect and abuse. You will receive the energy of gratitude tenfold in return.

And so it is.

*There is so much wanting to come through you. There is an
entire realm of infinite possibilities just waiting, on the brink
of your awareness. All that is left is for you to become present, and stay present, as you allow us to inspire PRESENT
moment action that is in alignment with this dream. You
often falter here. Your rational mind skips ahead to future
steps, layers of this dream that are way out of the present
moment, and because that image feels distant, unknown...
because there is a lack of clarity or understanding about this
step (because it is not present) you stutter. Energetically,
you hit a speed bump. The guidance you are receiving in the
present moment, the VERY next action you are being called
to take, is blocked. OR you allow your mind to guide you
into your memory banks, where you search for reassurance
that this new dream you are being called into will "work."
You can't find it there because you have yet to experience
it, so your rational mind tells you that it is not possible. You
feel doubt, uncertainty, even fear. This is all understandable
because your rational mind is past /future based and is NOT
the source of your unstoppable energy. Presence is what
is required of you to take one little step at a time. Step by
step, we will reach and stand together on the mountaintop
to survey all you have co-created with your unstoppable self,
because of the energy—the choice you made to cultivate
your sphere of presence.*

THE 6TH SPHERE OF WELLN
PRESENCE

Today you bring your unstoppableness into the very, very present moment.

The power of the present moment is so important to understand. There is a reason it is the 6th, final, Sphere of Wellness, because without it, truly you will experience more stoppable than unstoppable.

Your rational, logical mind is physiologically responsible for the past and future. This is the part of your awareness that stores all of your experiences up until now and then uses that information to project possible realities in the future. This is immensely valuable. We learn from our past and it is also vital that we prepare for the future— making sure we have enough wood chopped to make it through the winter, etc. AND, to balance this part of our awareness, we have our present-moment, intuitive, creative awareness that gives us the ability to receive inspiration in the moment and take action in the direction of the NEW dreams coming through us, without being blocked by the rational mind that wants to keep you safe, away from any unknown, and out of reach of any potential risk or failure.

Here's the call for you today: Bring yourself present, into the energy of you as the Unstoppable Dream, and ask yourself, "What can I do right NOW that will bring me one step closer to realizing this dream into my reality?" And if that step triggers your past/future thinking or if you feel any confusion or doubt, you are not present enough to receive just the very, very next thing you can do.

WARNING: *This very next step may seem too simple. It is not. It is what is right in front of you, available and accessible. And once you do that, the very NEXT step will be given to you.*

here's a sign that you want to send your attention into cultivating the energy of presence: overwhelm. Ever feel that? Right!? Overwhelm is the energy you are feeling to let you know that you are getting waaaaaaaayyyyy ahead of yourself. Bring your attention into the present moment. "What can I do right now that will bring me one inch, not one mile, closer to what I desire?"

Your Unstoppable Dream requires that your Sphere of Presence is nurtured and filled. When you drive your car, really drive. When you are in the shower, feel each drop of water. When you read, keep your thoughts from wandering. When you are making love, be right there 100% in the present moment. Remember, becoming Unstoppable simply requires nurturing your Metatron's Cube of vibrational well being. When these Spheres of Wellness are regularly attended to your unstoppableness will flow.

Let's fill up our Sphere of Presence now and feel into this present moment call to action.

Right now call in the awareness of you as a vibrational being. You as a vibrational being that is the union of the earth, material, physical energy and the cosmic energetic, vibrational, infinite energy. Because you are both of those things. You are the union, you are the infinite made visible.

Connect to the energies surrounding you. These spheres of wellness are like reservoirs that you can draw from, or tap into, at any moment. Feel them supporting you, creating a vibrational net all around you that creates a sense of lightness, the feeling of being supported and loved.

Connect now to your sphere of presence.

What does being present mean to you? Take a moment, close your eyes, and receive the energy of this space, this state of being.

What has your experience with the energy of presence been up until now? Is it, "Wow. I don't know if I've ever been present. I don't know the last time I've been present." Or maybe it's, "I am present when I'm outside in nature. I am present when I'm painting and I am present when...."

How does it feel for you to be present? Connect to that now.

Maybe there's an image that comes to you or a feeling. Maybe you feel it or you think it or you see it? Remember now what it is like when you're present.

If you've had any moments recently where you forgot about the current events and the headlines, that would be an example of being present.

What does it feel like when you realize that all the to-do's, the planning, the worries, have melted away? Can you feel this connection now between presence and alignment? There is a clarity, there is a singular focus in the energy of presence.

The opposite of presence may feel like a bucket with many, many holes punched in it. It is leaking its contents in never-ending streams. There is a scarcity, a fear of loss, of failure, of making a mistake as the energy leaks from the bucket.

When you are present, there are no leaks. You're in your power, you're in your strength in that moment, doing exactly what you're meant to do, not worrying about something that might possibly happen in the future, not allowing a label or an experience in the past to stop you from doing what you want.

You speak your truth, you hear your truth.

Can you feel that difference now?

Now ask your sphere of presence, "how full are you?"

The fuller it is, the more familiar this energy will be. Does it feel like, "Oh my Goddess, I need to go here more?" Or does it feel full? Like, "Okay, I'm doing this!" Or maybe you're understanding now why you do what you do (weeding the garden, knitting, driving, walking through the forest, writing in your journal...) because what you're actually doing is bringing yourself present.

Presence is very much the portal, or maybe it is this final, last thing that absolutely needs to be in place to be unstoppable. This is because whatever it is you want to experience next in your life, you haven't experienced up until now. It is going to involve some unknown. And we know that our logical, linear past future minds are physiologically programmed to resist all change. Presence is what allows your unstoppable nature to take the reins.

It is only in the present moment that we can experience alignment, that we can take steps, just one step, and then the very next step, towards whatever it is we're being called to create.

I invite you to connect to something new that you really want to experience in your life right now.

Maybe you really want to do a puzzle. Maybe you want to paint something. Maybe you want to start an online business. Maybe you want to start writing a book. Maybe you want to fix up your basement. Maybe you want to help families in need, fertilize your houseplants, or bake a cake. Whatever it is. Pick one thing now.

There is no hierarchy of choices. It can be doing a puzzle or it can be creating an online program or it can be learning sign language. Whatever it is, allow yourself to notice the first thing that comes to mind, or comes to your heart.

What do you really just feel? What do you desire? What do you want to experience? Or you could ask your unstoppable self, "What do you want to create through me next? What do we want to experience together?"

So what is that? Do you have something? It can even be something simple. If you're like, "Oh, I don't know," just use the equivalent of the puzzle example. Anything is fine for right NOW, right?

Write it below:

_____

_____

_____

_____

_____

_____

_____

_____

Now bring yourself into this present moment and honor this desire that you've chosen.

Even if it's the puzzle, or a bubble bath, there's a reason. There's something else that will come after even the simplest of actions, and you don't have to understand it all right now. In the present moment, you've been given this desire. You can feel it and you've chosen it. You've brought it into your space and now there's this element of action that joins this energy of presence, present action.

I want you to ask your unstoppable self, "What is the first step you want me to take? What is the first step you, who've given me this desire, who I know is wanting to create through me in this co-creative relationship, you who has everything I need, want me to take next? You see the big picture, but all that matters to me in this moment is the right now.

What do you want me to do now? What's the one step? I don't have to know step two or step three or step 100. What is the first step? And this is probably a very practical step. It's like, "Well, we need to get a puzzle Go to the store and buy a puzzle."

All you need to know is this first step. That's all that matters. It's all that exists. Nothing else is of consequence or nothing else needs to come into the picture except just this very next step. And does that next step feel doable?

Say you desire a bubble bath. The first step would be to plug the drain. Right? If you turn on the hot water before closing the drain, the tub won't fill. Then, turn on the water. You don't need to find the bubble bath yet, because it is impossible to take a bubble bath in an empty tub. See how easy this can be?

If it doesn't feel doable, that's fine, but that means you're still ahead a step or two. Simply ask, "What is before that step?"

We're talking about today, right now. So if it doesn't feel do-able today, say "Okay, good to know that step exists, but what's the step I can do now?" See how we can be so sneaky at keeping ourselves out of the present moment?

Now I want you to say to yourself out loud, "I am going to take this step now."

Feel into what is different. Is there a level of trust that maybe hasn't been there before? Is there an energy of clarity or alignment? Is there an energy of the weight of the world coming off your shoulders? Like, "Oh my gosh, I've been making this so difficult." What does that feel like? Like liberation or freedom? That's all I need to do!? It's that simple. Okay, I can do that.

That's how it should feel. "I can do that."

And even check, do you feel that? "I can do that."

If not, there's a step before that. It might be looking up on YouTube, how to.... Keep going until you get that very next step. And it feels so simple and easy. And then once you do that step, what do you do next? Repeat.

What is your VERY next step?

Write it below:

_____

_____

_____

_____

_____

_____

_____

_____

_____

_____

_____

_____

_____

Can you now see and feel how easy it is to get ahead of ourselves.? We can get so far ahead of the process that we've totally taken the present moment out of the equation. We're in this future unknown reality, already deciding that this future unknown reality is not reachable for us or not available to us. And so we don't take just that simple first, first, first step.

Now, when you feel that Unstoppable Dream energy inspiring your present moment you understand the call to focus on the very present moment and receive the VERY next step. Then, the next will be revealed as well. And the next...

This is the secret of anyone who is highly creative. Anyone who inspires the question within you, "I don't know how you do it all!" This person harnesses the power of presence.

If you are wondering what you can do NOW to cultivate this energy of presence, you can choose to do something totally new or different than you would normally. Doing ANYTHING new cultivates and stimulates your present moment awareness. After all, the present moment is all we really know for sure.

Right?

Namaste.

There is a powerful current of energy waiting to fill you up and generate your most authentic personal expression. It has become blocked in your culture because of your state of am-nesia. You forgot that love is the most powerful energy, the pinnacle of the energetic pyramid, and distracted yourself with achieving and producing. Today you will reconnect with this current and it will awaken within you a renewed sense of purpose and passion. So much of your dis-ease is caused by your lack of alignment. Allow yourself to refocus your at-tention on that which you love and feel yourself coming into your cente, where you are in your power.

THE MAGICAL THREAD BETWEEN LOVE & ALIGNMENT

Today you allow a spiraling helix of energy to flow from top to bottom, from love to alignment and back..

Throughout these pages, you are remembering how to care for yourself as a vibrational being. This means that you are releasing the material qualities of life on this planet as benchmarks of success and happiness and opening up more and more to the energetic qualities of living a joyful, fulfilled, inspired life. The game of life is such that we were initially taught that it was all about "getting to the cookie jar," when, in fact, it is all about the process, the journey, how you feel as you move forward, one square at a time, through the days of your life.

LOVE is the energy that will bring you into alignment. ALIGNMENT is the energy that signals you are in love with whatever you are experiencing. You can try to live in alignment without the energy of love dancing closely next to you, but you would be the first!

Connecting this magical thread, this helix of spiraling, glowing energy, between love and alignment in your energetic Metatron's Cube is infinite and multi-facted and it is also simple. The connection can be made with one question:

What have you always loved to do?

What has always captured your attention and inspired boundless curiosity?

Who you are at your core, without any input from anyone else, can be reignited by reconnecting to the simple things that you have always loved, even since you were a child. Here is a fun exercise I created to identify my "core values," which is another way of reengaging the energy of alignment.

Let's Explore Your 3 Most Significant Memories

What is your very first memory as a child?

Take a moment to breathe into your heart. Feel everything but the present moment melting away. You are a child again. Allow your subconscious mind to offer to you right now your earliest childhood memory. Resist the urge to judge it. Whatever comes to mind right now is perfect.

Write this memory below:

_____

_____

_____

_____

_____

_____

_____

_____

_____

_____

Now, what is your next most significant memory? Maybe it was something memorable between the ages of 5-10 because of how fun this experience was or because of how sad or challenging this experience was. Either is fine.

Write it below:

_____

_____

_____

_____

_____

_____

_____

_____

_____

_____

_____

_____

_____

Finally, one more significant memory from your school age years. This could be any time between ages 10-18. What comes to mind? Simply receive the memory right now.

Write it below:

_____

_____

_____

_____

_____

_____

_____

_____

_____

_____

My first memory was putting together the swingset with my dad just before my brother was born. I was 2 months or so shy of turning 3. I remember being on the grass in the backyard. It was just me and my dad. He was happy. The swingset was super exciting. We were having fun. Look back at your first memory. What is the predominant energy of this experience? For me it was FUN. I know FUN to be absolutely one of my core values.

I also had a client whose first memory was standing in her crib crying for her mother. That memory connected her to a long memory of trying to get her mother's attention. Not a "fun" memory. With deeper inquiry she realized that what she was desiring in that moment as a baby in the crib was connection. She also realized that as a mother herself, she had always made sure to be extra attentive to her children. She did not want them to feel the lack of connection that she had. So one of her greatest core values was connection. Positive or negative memories can each guide you to one of your core values.

My second memory was in kindergarten when I contracted scarlet fever and chickenpox, back to back. I was really sick. I was out of school for a little over a month. It was the worst case of chickenpox my 70-something old doctor had ever seen and the Scarlet Fever rash inspired a midnight trip to the emergency room for a chest x-ray. It was that kind of scary sickness. I can still remember feeling SO destroyed. I remember my neighbor mom having me over for a tea party when I was covered with chicken pox so her 5 kids would get chicken pox (younger I guess was better) and I was exhausted. I couldn't wait to go home. My parents moved the tv into my room and I got to eat milkshakes every day! (I even had chicken pox in my mouth!) After that month and after my scabs went away and the kids stopped teasing me, even more magical things happened! My family celebrated with a trip to Great America, the Six Flags amusement park about an hour away and I got a new dress!

When I was given the assignment in 4th grade to write about my best life experience, I wrote about scarlet fever and chickenpox. I learned that when you survive deep, dark experiences you are rewarded with shiny, sparkly experiences. I had been initiated into the power of contrast and the joy that results when we can rise above the "illness" and catch hold of that silver lining. I have always valued, as a result, life's challenges. Coming out of them, I instantly look for the gift. What did I learn? What do I now know I am NOT? How am I stronger, wiser, more compassionate? I love the roller coaster ride, the ups and downs. I teach now that we learn through contrast. Contrast. Optimism. My Polly-Anna self is highly valued.

My third significant memory was 5th grade. I was SO in my zone in 5th grade. I loved my teacher and the feeling was mutual. Most significantly, I was the only kid in the class who had two desks—the kind that lift up to reveal storage for your papers. It had the peninsula of desktop that reached around your right side (not sure what left-handed students did) to provide a rest for your writer's arm. Remember those? On both of my desks I had taped white drawing paper to that right side, taking full advantage of that peninsula of vertical space. On the top of the paper I always wrote "Doodleos" (doo-dle-ee-os). Below that is where I drew, or doodled and the bottom section, the tip of the peninsula was separated by a border design so that my visitors could doodle there. It was my first "art center." My core self, my most aligned, authentic self has always valued creativity.

Look back on your three memories. What was the predominant feeling, or energy, in each one. If it was a "negative" feeling or energy, what is the flipside of that energy? If you felt abandoned, how do you now value loyalty or being truly present for the people in your life?

Write down your core values below:

_____

_____

_____

_____

_____

_____

_____

_____

_____

_____

_____

_____

Now, here is the super fun part. To nurture this flow of energy between your Sphere of Love and your Sphere of Alignment, do more that is in alignment with your core values. For me it is: 1) Do more of anything that I find FUN, 2) Do something different, something that challenges me, something that contrasts my normal, and 3)Create something, anything. Get creative!

When I do ANYTHING that is in alignment with those three things, I am becoming a vibrational being that has a bright, glowing, flowing, spiraling helix of loving aligned energy flowing through me and rippling out into the world. It becomes easier and easier to release that which is no longer in alignment and to focus on that which you love.

Here is more good news: Whatever is NOT in alignment in your life does not require your direct attention now.

For example, let's say you dislike your job. It is not in alignment with your core values, to put it mildly. And you need the income right now. Do not preoccupy yourself with how to quit your job. DO preoccupy yourself with as many things that you love, that are in alignment with your core values. FILL UP your Spheres of Love and Alignment first. Make that your top priority. Then, in however many weeks, months, somehow your job will transform. You will find another one, or you will get laid off and be forced to find something else, or perhaps something will shift at work to make it more enjoyable. Because you will have raised your vibration from doing more of what you love, the job you don't love can NOT stay in alignment and it will have to detach from your vibrational being.

I just had a vision of a space station releasing a satellite into space. You know that image? You can almost imagine the switch being flipped, and you are looking out the window of the space station, you see the satellite detach and float away effortlessly to find its own orbit.

When you nurture the connection between love and alignment, allowing what you love to dominate your attention and time, bringing you into the feeling of alignment, authenticity and purpose, anything in your life that is not harmonious with those energies will simply detach and float away into "space."

It's not about fixing, forcing, worrying, or trying. It IS about redirecting your attention and intention towards that which you love.

In even the smallest tasks of your day, ask yourself, "How would I love to do this the most?" What kind of exercise would feel the best right now. "I said I was going to run each day, but I feel like stretching." Do yoga today for a change.

"I have chicken out for dinner, but I really feel like pancakes." Make pancakes.

"I love the scent of lavender." Add lavender to your dish soap or your bath. Dab lavender on your glorious body.

BE the union of love and alignment and watch as those energies expand and expand in your life.

And so it is.

You are now ready to release the energies of blame, or being a victim, of failure, of guilt, of anger... From your crystalline space within the union of above and below, surrounded by everything you need to thrive and prosper in this lifetime, you are ready to forgive. You are now transmuting the energy of forgiveness into gratitude. Everyone who has ever crossed, hurt, violated, or betrayed you now come into focus as your greatest allies. These are the souls who volunteered to provide you the lessons you desired to learn. It is because contrast is what propels our learning forward that you have experienced these dark spaces in your life. "Love your enemies." They come, cloaked in darkness, that you may be given the opportunity to choose to shine your light. You experience deceit so that you can know deeply the power of honesty. You experience violence so that you can be a warrior for peace, a peace that radiates from deep within you, a peaceful place you discovered first amidst the struggle. You experience hate so that you can love that much more powerfully. You have been broken so that in the process of repairing yourself you would become your strongest self. Perhaps forgiveness has challenged you because what is truly wanting to come forth is gratitude. What if...?

THE MAGICAL THREAD BETWEEN COMPASSION & GRATITUDE

Today you transform lower energies into the highest energies..

One of my favorite analogies is between life and the improv stage. I remember when a dear friend first offered this to me. When you are on an improv stage, one of the golden rules is that you have to say "Yes!" to everything. As the dialogue shifts, and the scene transforms, you are not permitted to say, "I don't want to do that." You go with it. That is the nature of improv, the spontaneity, the uncontrollable process that calls you into roles that you may have never even imagined.

Imagine that on the stage one day the scene shifts and your fellow actor becomes mean and hateful. You are catapulted into a scenario in which you are victimized, minimalized, or mistreated. You respond in the moment, matching the "story" being co-created there on that stage. Within minutes, the scene shifts once again...perhaps now you are WonderWoman, flying in her invisible jet, or a puppy clamouring for attention. At the end of the improv session you walk off the stage and say to your partner, "Wow! You rocked that villain role! You were super mean. I really felt scared! Good job!" Or maybe, "You took me to a place in my acting that I had never experienced before. I got raw and really felt the scene. Thank you."

You wouldn't hold whatever they acted out on stage against them, would you?

What if this life was like an improv stage.

What if these "characters" in your life who have hurt you, were simply playing a role to inspire change, transformation, resolve, personal power, or wisdom in your life? Are you a better mother because you "never want to do what your mother did?" Are you a better partner because of your parents relationship? Are you more compassionate to others because you have experienced moments, days, weeks, years... when you powerfully desired an iota of compassion from someone dear to you? Do you shower those around you with words of praise because you never heard those words from that person in your life? Who else has hurt you? As a result, what is the contrasting experience that you have also celebrated? What have you learned because of their actions? Now, can you feel into how you are stronger, wiser, more loving... as a result? Now surround that in gratitude and send this ally compassion.

I am so grateful I am not...

I am so grateful I learned how not to...

I am so grateful because I appreciate _____ more than most.

I am so grateful because if not for so-and-so I would not have...

I can feel compassion for the people in my life who have hurt me now because I understand the gift I have received. May their life journeys have led them to opportunities to forgive themselves and find self-compassion.

This is not easy. And it is truth. Gratitude is the highest path one can take in releasing low energy from any past experience. And it will raise your vibration around any low vibrational experience in your past. It will provide you personal power that has been transmuted from a shade of victimhood.

Gratitude is a powerful medicine that has the potential to release low vibrational energies being held in these past experiences, raising your vibration now, expanding your Sphere of Compassion and releasing that stuck, dense energy from within your field.

In 2010, I taught a quantum painting workshop at The Esalen Institute with Dr. Christine Ranck. We explored together how the mind does not distinguish between real and imagined events, as explained by Quantum Physics.

What I learned is that it is possible to re-visit painful memories from our past, really take yourself back to that time and space, feeling it, remembering the details: what you were wearing, what they were wearing, etc. and re-write the "script." You can recreate a past experience in your mind and then imagine it happening differently. It could be anything from SuperMan swooping in, punching out the "bad guy" and carrying you away to safety, or you standing up for yourself and saying what you wished you had said.

What I found personally, and others in the group concurred, that the negative experience that I redirected in my mind, that had up until then held so much sadness for me, just dissolved. The energy in my chest that used to come up, and the tears that would begin to well in my eyes, when I took myself back to this memory from 7th grade, simply disappeared. It was replaced with a healthy detachment. It took its proper place waaaaayyyy in my past and, with my new story in which I stood up for myself instead of cowering and crying, I even felt waves of accomplishment for "handling the situation" in my power—so powerful is my mind that it had literally transformed the experience into one for which I could feel gratitude. Your mind is this powerful too.

Want to try?

*Pick an experience, maybe not your most traumatic, but one that you can remember that feels heavy and sad for you. Maybe it is a relationship with a friend that ended abruptly in a disagreement or a boss firing you and you want to say the words you wished you had said to her. Did a kid tease you when you were little or did a teacher ever put you down? Something like that. Do you have it?

Now REALLY remember this experience. Feel it like you are right there. Look at the people you are with. Look down at your clothes, where you are standing or sitting. Was it cold or warm? What was the weather doing? Was it night or day? Feel it deeply. Re-create the scene in your mind. Now, imagine you doing whatever it is differently so that this scene plays out in your favor. Maybe you call the friend back and you are both able to share and forgive. Maybe you let that boss know exactly what you've been holding back forever and they receive it, or they change their mind, or...? What do you wish had happened in this experience? Do that now in your imagination. Be the hero. Be your wise woman self. Be more compassionate. Be stronger. Stick to your guns. Say the words. Do that in your mind now.

What have you learned now from this exercise? How did it feel to speak your truth or draw the line or...? Can you now understand this event from a different angle? What did you not understand that you now understand? Is that valuable to you now? Can you use this benefit of hindsight to create change in any of your current experiences? Do you see how you have done other things differently, better, as a result of this past event?

Now, imagine looking at the person(s) from your past that hurt you. They are right here with you. Can you say, "Thank you."

I am grateful that you created for me the opportunity to learn...

Thank you.

Thank you.

I am grateful.

And so it is.

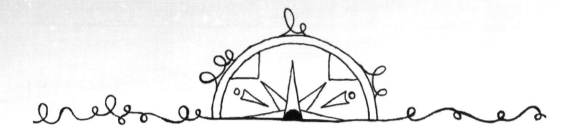

A small child needs rules and boundaries to the extent that will keep them physically safe from harm. They have not yet learned the importance of looking both ways before crossing a street, nor that fire burns or icy walkways are slippery. Their innocence in the ways of the world are balanced by the wisdom of their guardians. On the other side of this truth is the super power that is their innocence. They have yet to absorb the limiting beliefs and collective stories that will inevitably fill their consciousness and stop them on the brink of their unknown. When you remember the power of presence, you reclaim your connection to your innocence and can leap into the unknown courageously because you choose in that moment of the leap to suspend the stories that told you you couldn't.

THE MAGICAL THREAD BETWEEN COURAGE & PRESENCE

Today you reclaim your innocence.

The kingdom of heaven belongs to the childlike, the innocent. Remember this teaching? The energy of innocence is often referenced in spiritual teachings, and I used to connect this word to other words like naivete, simpleness, and foolishness. Then, one day, not so long ago, I got it. The innocence spoken of is unburdened with past failures or shortcomings, which has forgotten others' expectations and the roles and labels assumed. Innocence can exist for any of us in the present moment. In the NOW, we are not our past. We are not limited by our experience up until now. We are not jaded by past disappointments or skeptical of the probability of desired futures. We are simply here now.

In the present moment, you can reclaim your innocence.

How does this help you to be more courageous?

When we feel a lack of courage, we are hesitant to take steps into the unknown. We are allowing our past to project undesired images of the future, and so we stop instead of leaping.

When your Sphere of Courage is feeling low, ask if your state of being when you are not in alignment with courage is present-oriented or past-future oriented. Are you allowing your past to hold you back? Does the fear of a future in which the net does NOT appear post-leap have control over you or not?

What would it take courage to do in your life right now?

I'm not going to tell you that you HAVE to do this thing right now, so feel free, to be honest with yourself.

There is a fear surrounding this dream, this vision, right?

What is the fear-based on? Where does it come from? What past experience is being triggered at the thought of doing this thing? What fear of the future is dominating your awareness?

You learn from your past, and learning from your past, the "good and the bad," is unavoidable. AND it is the "baggage," the heavy energies, the guilt, the fear, the worry that you have picked up along your path that is now making you too heavy to make that leap. You have to set down the baggage. You can choose presence. From that present moment, with NO baggage and zero attention focused on your past, you have reclaimed your innocence. You believe you can fly...and so you leap!

Follow this thread of thought...

"If I was in a state of innocence right now, I would still believe...

I would still wish...

I would still want...

If I brought myself completely present, with complete amnesia of whatever has caused me to fear, to hesitate, to stop..., I would courageously leap into _____!"

If no one had ever told you that you weren't good enough, not smart enough, not talented enough... what would you do?

When you nurture your Sphere of Presence, you will find yourself connecting to and feeling the energy of courage more and more in your life. You will naturally be guided, when on the brink of the leap, to breathe into your center, to release the worry and doubt, and to focus on all the ways you are prepared. Then, watch out, world! Here I come! Wheeeeeeeee!

Cowabunga!!!!

You are so courageous!

And so it is.

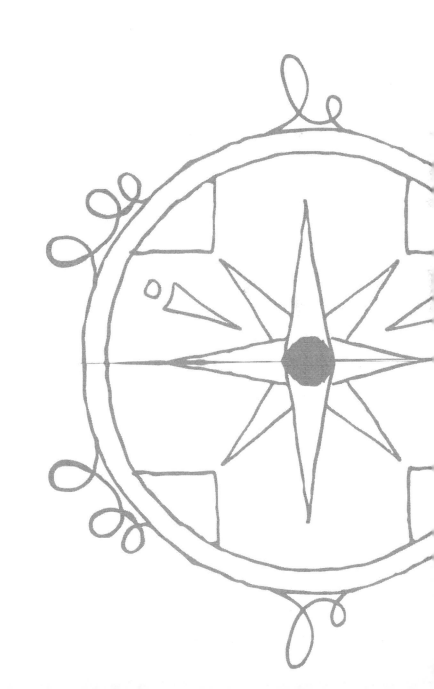

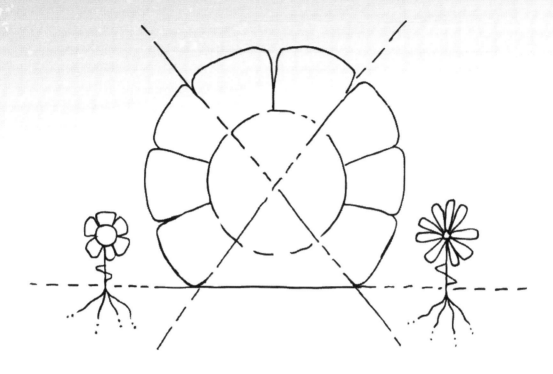

You have the simplest and yet the most powerful example of how creative you are and how to focus that creativity right outside your door. Your garden provides you with a magical mirror of how you create and how you often misdirect your creative energies. From the seed to the fruit or flower to the winter bareness, the entire natural process of growing a garden mirrors how you can align with your most Unstoppable You. Plant the seeds you desire. Nurture those seeds with love. Weed out what you don't want to grow. Allow time for the ripening. Feel gratitude for the harvest and allow the winter's rest.

YOUR SPHERE OF LOVE—
GROWING A GARDEN

Today you realign with the co-creative relationship you have with Gaia.

You know that feeling of extreme excitement, when something enters your field of perception and its energy ripples through you, bringing a sense of joyful anticipation and excitement? "Ooooh! I want to do that! ...go there! ...learn that! ...see that! How cool!"

There is an instant surge of positive energy, a resonance that just feels so good. It's yours!

Then, whether it is an hour later, a day later, or a week... you give up on whatever got you so excited. "Practicalities" come into your field of perception. Your rational mind reminds you of all the unknowns, the times you tried something new and "failed," etc. Or you start whatever process sparked that joy within you, and then the energy just seemed to dwindle each day. You've been given an Unstoppable Dream, but you are not able to sustain the vibration in order to hold onto it. The high vibration you experienced in that "ah-ha!" moment has been replaced by the lower vibration energies of doubt and worry.

That initial "ah-ha!" that excitement for the "dream" that generated such a surge in energy was the "seed." In that moment of recognition, your dream contained within it the blueprint for its fruition. It just needed you to claim it, plant it, nurture it, tend to its needs, and then to reap its harvest, experience its fruition. But the seed never got "planted," or you "planted" it but didn't water it. Or maybe it even sprouted, but it never received the light of your full intention, and it withered and died or got choked out by all the "weeds" of doubt and fear.

Or, perhaps, you planted the seed and found yourself upset that it wasn't "growing" quicker. You got turned on, excited, and you wanted the dream to manifest NOW. Trust me, I speak from experience. How easy is it to impose our time frame onto our "dreams?"

"It's not working."

"We will see how it goes."

"I hope it works."

I hear these phrases all the time. It? There is no "it." There is only YOU. If you DECIDE it is going to work, it will. It may not "work" on your timeline, but it will work when you choose to see your dream through to "harvest" NO MATTER WHAT.

Let's break down this garden analogy into four layers. Each of them is fueled by your Sphere of LOVE, not doubt, uncertainty, indecision, lack...LOVE. When you LOVE a dream that has just been given to you, and you continue to nurture that dream with LOVE, however long, however much love it requires, you will enjoy the "harvest."

Layer 1: Intent

This is the seed. When you are planting a garden, you CHOOSE the seeds you want to plant, based on the experience that this seed promises in your future. If you don't want eggplant, you don't plant eggplant. Right? When you love and desire juicy, fresh tomatoes growing in your garden, you plant tomato seeds. You understand that within those teeny tiny seeds is everything it needs to grow into a big tomato plant, laden with round, ripe tomatoes. You know it will get there as long as you plant it in the dirt, water, and care for it. After all your nurturing, you get to pick the tomatoes off the branches. Within each seed is a blueprint for the grown plant.

AND you are not the tomato plant. You are given the seed, and the seed needs your help to get in the ground and create the conditions for it to grow that are in alignment with the seed, but the seed has everything it needs within. You don't have to teach it how to grow tomatoes. It won't yield bananas if you don't do something "right." You are its lovely assistant. You are the gardener, not the garden itself.

How does that connect you to your dream? Can you understand that when you get that flash of insight, the "ah-ha!" moment of excitement, of high vibration recognition of something that you want to experience in your life, that everything you and your dream needs to manifest in your life is there, contained within that seed of energy that you have just received? And you choose to guide this dream into existence because you LOVE the idea of it! Right? You don't choose a dream that you don't like. "Gee, I really want to get that job that sounds super boring and tedious." Haha. Right? No. You choose dreams that you LOVE. The LOVE is the signal that it is for you to dream into reality. So you choose it and set the INTENT to be the channel, the vehicle, through which this dream can become a memory for you, a part of your life experience. Intent, combined with the resolution to see this dream through to "harvest," is all you need to begin embodying you as the Unstoppable Dream. You now understand that your dream has everything it needs, just like the seed, to grow and bare fruit in your life. Next step in the journey is simply to nurture your dream.

Layer 2: Nurture

Now that you have chosen your dream/seed, it has been "planted." It has found a home, a nest within your energy field. And it is there that it intends to grow and expand into physical reality. And it still needs your help.

A seed won't even break through the surface of the soil if it does not receive water and warmth. What is the equivalent for your dream? What does it need next? Does it require you to learn something new? To sign up for something? To call someone? To apply for...? Does it want to be written down? Shared with others? What are all the things you can do to create "fertile ground" within which your dream can begin to grow?

Keeping it to yourself won't do it. Ignoring it won't help it. Burying it in all the reasons why it probably will never grow anyway will certainly kill it. Do you see?

What is the LIGHT it needs?

What is the WATER it needs?

What are the NUTRIENTS it needs?

Focus your loving energy on all the ways you can support the growth of your dream/seed.

TRUST. "It isn't working." Your seed hasn't broken through the surface of your garden yet. It is not visible. You have no idea if it is still there, if it has died, or if it was a bum seed. You begin to doubt.

As I write this, we are a couple of months into our new "Corona World," and I have planted A LOT of seeds in my garden during this time. My dill seeds took FOREVER to reveal their delicate green shoots to me. The basil seeds still haven't broken the surface of the soil. The carrots did finally sprout, and I think I see a couple of beets, but I'm not sure. What I experienced for the first time is that seeds (typically) will germinate when THEY are ready. Some seeds needed some warm days and lots of sun to germinate. Some needed the rain. They know when to germinate because they may get nipped by frost or not receive enough light if they do so too soon. I have learned to trust, to surrender to the wisdom of the seed. I continue to nurture even though these seeds are not growing according to my timeline.

My third book, *Rise Above*, was "slated" by my logical mind to be published in 2016. I had created an online program for 2015, and each month I created a chapter in the book to share with my students. (BTW, that is how I nurtured that dream. I knew if I created an audience that expected a chapter each week, I would be sure to write it!) So it "made sense" that it would be completed, published, and delivered into their hands in 2016. That was my timeline, not the dream/book timeline.

As it turned out, 2016 was the end of a 9-year cycle (2 + 0 + 1 + 6 = 9). I ended up teaching about this in December 2016 and, in the process, aligned with the "blueprint" of the "seed" that was my book, *Rise Above*. Publishing a book in a "9 year" would be like trying to plant the seeds in your garden in the fall, at the end of the growing cycle. Publishing the same book in one year, 2017, is like planting in the spring, after the chance of frost has passed. If I had not trusted my sense of timing, making it okay within myself that I would not publish the book in 2016, I would have been paddling against the current to force its launch into the world. I mean, I had promised the finished text in 2016 to the 100+ people who had joined my 2015 program. Right? Trust.

Layer 3: Trust

Trust that if your dream isn't making itself more visible or tangible to you, or if you do not see the results you expected, there is simply a different timeline in play, and you can, and you want to, trust that timing. After all, the dream knows best. It is not really YOUR dream, with your timeline contained within its blueprint. It is a dream that has filtered through the layers, the dimensions, infinite space and time, and found you to birth it into reality according to its own blueprint. It's a tomato seed that will become a tomato, not a banana. Let it do its thing and trust its timing.

Layer 4: Surrender

Now your seed has been planted, and you have nurtured it, so it has grown, blossomed, and is about to bear fruit. It is vibrant, colorful, and can be seen by all. Your dream is about to come to fruition. It's time to connect to the energy of surrender. Why? Remember that quote by Marianne Williamson that our true fear is not about failing, but about being successful? We fear our greatness. We fear being seen. What if I can't live up to the dream? What if people see me for who I really am?! This is the imposter syndrome.

EXACTLY BECAUSE our dream has been "given" to us.

EXACTLY BECAUSE our dream is also the dream of the Universe, we can shrink back right at the moment of expansion.

This resistance to the step of surrendering is also known as self-sabotage. Unconsciously, we can protect ourselves from the unknown world that lies on the other side of our dream's fruition by stopping. We find excuses to postpone the "launch." At the last minute, we decide that instead of tomatoes, we really wanted to plant green beans. So we pull up the tomato plants that are almost ready to be harvested and decide to use that space next spring for beans because, after all, that is what we really wanted. Ooooh, this energy can be so sneaky. You really, truly believe, and you will defend it to others, that you really wanted beans. Beans are your destiny. Beans are what you have always loved the most.

Okay, are you feeling the tough LOVE coming through these words? No judgment. Been there, done that. And how true is this? Do you feel it? How do you self-sabotage? It's okay. You are still AH-mazing. And let's dig in here.

Take a moment to connect to what you love, what you want to love even more in your life. Maybe a "dream" comes to mind that you intended, nurtured, experienced some trust, and then sabotaged it. You stopped short of realizing the dream.

COMPASSION. Remember our Sphere of Compassion, self-compassion. We have all experienced a shade of this frequency.

And, here is the antidote...

When you get to that edge, the threshold, where just steps away you can see those big, ripe tomatoes, the fruition of your dream is right there, and you start to feel yourself resist, the idea comes to mind, "I think I want beans," what you are called to do next is RAISE your vibration. This fear of your greatness, the fear of being revealed as the imposter, as a fake, or not as "good" as your dream is calling you to be, has lowered your vibration.

Unstoppable Soul, receiver of dreams, can you now focus your loving energy on what you love about your dream?

What do you love about what you have experienced up until now?

What can you do right now that you LOVE?

Tap into your Sphere of Love. Raise your vibration. Invite in your Sphere of Compassion, imagine how many other people in the world are feeling hesitant at the edge of their own dream come true. Send them COURAGE. Breathe in love, compassion, courage... Reconnect to the alignment that you have experienced in this "gardening" process, send gratitude to the seed, the light, the water... and stay present.

Right NOW, what can you do to allow this dream, these beautiful tomatoes, to come to fruition? You got this. You got this because you remember now that you are the vehicle, the union of matter and light, and it is ONLY through you that this dream can manifest into our physical reality. You love it. You are Unstoppable.

And so it is.

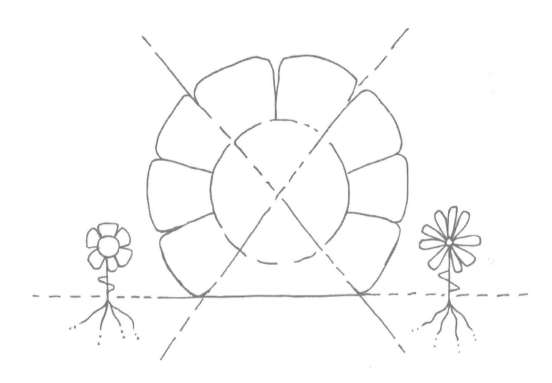

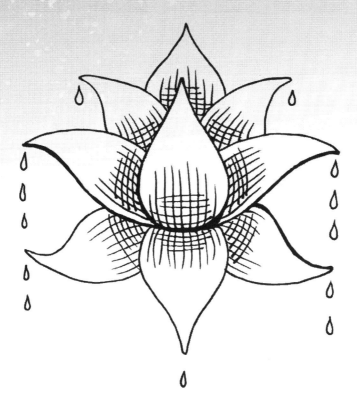

You have disappointed yourself at times. You have done things under the influence of an intoxicant, under the influence of another, or under the influence of a temptation. You have let others down. You have let yourself down. You have lied. You have cheated. You have stolen. You have judged yourself and others. You have discriminated against yourself and others. You have been stubborn. You have been angered and have said hurtful things. You have doubted yourself and others. You have killed another's hopes and dreams. You have tried to take more than you deserve. You have hidden truth from a situation. You have... All of these experiences have been SO THAT you could ultimately practice self-compassion. You are not able to experience self-forgiveness until you do something to require your own forgiveness. You can not understand another's suffering until you have suffered your own harshness or unforgiveness. You came to be fully human, to feel the call, and still ask for the "cup" to be passed on to another. Can you see your shadows, the times and experiences that you wouldn't want to share with anyone else, from the perspective of a warrior who left it all on the field? You didn't come here to be perfect, you ARE perfection. You came here to be perfect at forgiving yourself. You came here to be the perfect example of compassion turned inward.

YOUR SPHERE OF COMPASSION— SHADOW'S ROLE

Today you take back power from within the shadows.

One of my favorite spiritual practices is inspired by the Buddhist Tonglen practice. It creates an opportunity for me to be a blessing to others in the midst of my own pity party.

When I am sad, angry, upset, worried... I feel alone. I don't see anyone helping me. I feel like the world is against me, like what is available to everyone else isn't available to me. That can all shift with one simple question.

"Hmmm... I wonder how many other people on this planet are feeling sad, angry, upset, worried...?

Probably hundreds. No, probably thousands or even millions of people are feeling exactly the way I am feeling right now."

Then, you tap into the feeling or the energy of thousands, or millions of people feeling sad... Feel them. Imagine a young woman feeling sad and alone. Imagine a little child feeling worried or angry. Imagine a young father not able to care for his family, or an old woman feeling helpless and weak. Do you feel their sorrow?

Ask yourself, "How would I want them to feel right now? What would I wish for them? What would I bless them with if I could?

I would want them to feel loved, to feel safe, to feel secure. I would want them to feel supported and cared for. I would want them to feel appreciated and surrounded by options and hope. Hope. I would want for them right now to feel hopeful."

When the feeling you would wish for others "lands" in your heart, generate that feeling within you. Connect to all the ways and all the times you have felt hopeful. What are all the reasons you can feel hopeful right now? Feel hopeful. Be the energy of hope. Allow this energy to build, to expand and to begin to glow within you. Imagine this energy getting bigger and bigger, expanding from within you to outside of you—surrounding yourself with a bubble of hope. Allow this bubble to grow bigger and bigger. "I feel so hopeful. I feel so hopeful."

Imagine this energy of hope spreading out from your home, blanketing the land all around you, your entire town, the country you live in, the continent... And then imagine it overflowing and spilling over the entire planet. A tsunami of hope energy bathing the entire planet. Imagine people everywhere lifting their heads, a flash of an idea that gives them hope illuminating their awareness, a friend stopping by to ask if they can help. Imagine waves of hope bathing households, alleyways and places of work with its sense of possibility and support.

Now, how do you feel? Hopeful, right?

Everyone has failed. Everyone has done things for which they have experienced the energy of shame or guilt. Everyone. I have. You have. We all have.

Would you forgive me for shoplifting as a teenager? For lying to my husband? For not doing the best I could in any situation? I've done all these things and more.

Can you do the same for yourself? Imagine this shadow part of you, the you that did this thing, coming into the light. Imagine her head is down, her eyes sad. Take her face in your hands. Raise her eyes to meet your's. Say to her, "I understand. I forgive you. I don't blame you. You were doing the best you could. You sacrificed yourself so that I could have this moment right now of radical self-compassion."

Now... Now... Now, how much easier is it to be the energy of compassion for another?

Can you feel and send compassion to that person who lied to or cheated you? Can you forgive the person who said that...? Can you feel compassion for the human that is the person trying and failing, for not believing they are worthy, for hiding, or deceiving another? Can you allow yourself to be human? Will you accept my humanness? Will you love this journey called life exactly because it guides us into the shadows so that we can experience the light of compassion?

And so it is.

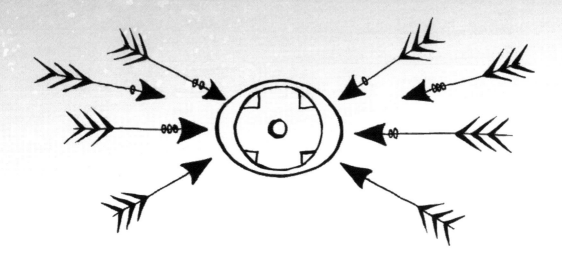

You think your world is in conflict, forces fighting against each other, debating and undermining. It is a mirror. Go within your own inner world and receive the awareness of your own inner conflicts. Where are you divided, fighting against yourself? At once you are desiring something to come into your life experience while simultaneously throwing up barriers and roadblocks so that it can never truly enter. You think, "I would so love..." and then the majority of your consciousness is exploring all the reasons and ways you will never experience the fruition of this desire. Is it so hard to imagine your inner world being one that is in constant harmony with your heart's desires? There is a world available to you within that cheers you on, that looks for all the reasons and ways your heart's desires are rushing towards you, like a raging river in spring. Your desires are tripping over themselves in their eagerness to be experienced THROUGH you. Today let's activate this potential reality so you can choose it... or not.

Day 21

YOUR SPHERE OF COURAGE— EXPLORING COHERENT CONSCIOUSNESS

Today you call in your next level of personal coherence, within and without.

We know courage is about following your heart. The root cause of our dissonance within is that we have been taught to honor logic and rational thinking, which often contradicts the desires of your heart. And we know the tremendous wisdom and energy of our heart center. We know that our body is one of our most refined instruments for perceiving the truth and attracting to us that which we require to experience our heart's desires in this physical experience.

It is subtle. Our undermining of our own desires is very subtle because our worries and excuses are so logical. Will you accept now the truth that life is not logical? It does not unfold along a predictable, linear, practical, rational path. It twists and turns, and loop-d-loops through multiple dimensions and a myriad of realities. Every choice you make, every word you speak is spinning universes of reality within and around you. You weave a life experience of struggle and dissonance when you sacrifice your heart's wisdom for that of your mind...up until now.

Breathe deeply into your heart. Feel how that breath expands your entire being.

Breathe into your heart.

Breathe into your heart.

Now try to breathe into your mind. Breathe into your head.

What does that feel like?

Breathe into your heart.

Breathe into your brain.

Your heart radiates.

Your mind is a dead end.

Feel the difference.

Your heart only knows love and possibility. And it has the power to transmute your doubts and fears because it also knows that it is through contrast that you learn and expand. It can wrap any fear you have, any old limiting belief or story that is blocking the fruition of your heart's desire, in radical acceptance and unconditional love. It is through the experience of polarity, of dissonance, that you remember the beauty and truth of harmony.

You are now being the experience of harmony for yourself every day.

You are now surrounding yourself in every moment with your heart's wisdom.

You are now supporting yourself with encouraging, possibility-illuminating, and self-loving thoughts, words, ideas, conversations.

You now see how the contrasts and the conflicts in your life have given you the knowing from which you can now wisely choose coherence of mind, body and spirit.

You now expand your ability to discern those desires that are coming from your Unstoppable, Infinite Self and how to surround these visions with a clear tunnel of luminescence, love and anticipation of their inevitable manifestation into your life.

You no longer fight against yourself.

You no longer struggle to feel worthy of being someone who receive. I receive. I receive.

I receive all the wisdom I need to realize the fruition of my heart's desires.

I receive all the self-love and self-acceptance I need to realize the fruition of my heart's desires.

I receive all the magical synchronicities and coincidences I need to realize the fruition of my heart's desires.

I receive all the allies, seen and unseen that I need to realize the fruition of my heart's desires.

I receive all the wisdom I need to realize the fruition of my heart's desires.

I receive all the time and physical resources I need to realize the fruition of my heart's desires.

I receive all the financial support I need to realize the fruition of my heart's desires.

I receive all the energy and physical strength I need to realize the fruition of my heart's desires.

I receive all the confidence and conviction I need to realize the fruition of my heart's desires.

I receive all the levels of coherent consciousness I need to realize the fruition of my heart's desires.

And so it is.

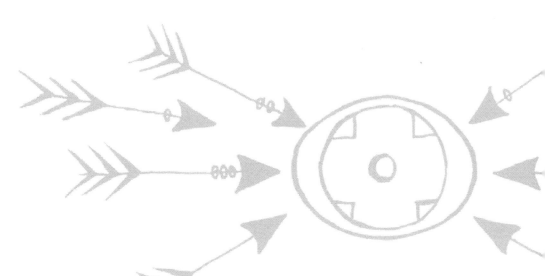

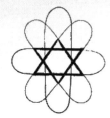 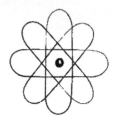 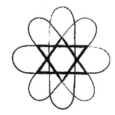

You are ready now to dissolve the distraction of matter and, in its place, expands your awareness of the truth that everything is energy. When you recognize this universal truth, energy becomes a medium that you can direct, guide, and from which you can create your highest physical experience. Like energy attracts like energy. From this fact, you can move through your life magnetizing to you everything you need and everything you desire, in harmony in each moment. Energy exists before matter. Energy is what connects you to the void, the field of pure potentiality. It allows you to create in the ethers, where anything is possible, and witness your visions manifest into form. Be the energy you want to attract. Send your energy in the direction of your desires. Align with the energies that bring you joy. You can do this more powerfully starting now.

YOUR SPHERE OF ALIGNMENT— LIVING IN A WORLD OF ENERGY

Today you remember that the most powerful matrix you can live within is the one that recognizes that everything is energy.

Imagine that in front of you are two doors. All that exists is these two doors until a voice introduces you to their purpose. You hear this invitation.

"I am going to describe to you what lies behind each of these doors and then you get to choose which one to step through. Behind door number one is you living your life with any kind of material possession that you want. Your every wish is granted regarding matter. Want a ski boat? Yours. Want a big house on the ocean? Yours. Cars, jewelry, travel...it's all yours. This is your world with every material wish of yours granted.

Behind door number two is you living your life bathed in any kind of energy you desire. However you desire to feel is yours in infinite abundance. Joy? It's yours. Peace? Yours. Happiness, elation, gratitude, inspiration, fulfillment...it's all yours. Behind door number two you can live in a constant state of bliss." Feel into this reality.

Then, feel into the reality of unlimited matter, things and stuff.

Which do you choose: A life of infinite joy or a life of infinite things?

Breathe deeply.

Which would you choose? Behind door number one is no promise of happiness. Behind door number two there is no promise of physical comforts.

And, if you are feeling completely joyful and happy, could you also feel in need or deprived in any way?

There is a profound liberation being offered to you right now. When you recognize that you live in a world of energy you get access to all the joy, peace, happiness that you could possibly desire because it is within you that you generate energy. You don't need anything on the material plane to nurture and radiate high states of emotion and feeling. You are remembering now that life is an inside out job. The greatest journey does not lie through a world of matter, it lies within the twists and turns, mountains, valleys and oceans of awareness within you.

If you desire financial abundance you can work hard to create it in the world of matter or you can generate the feeling of abundance by noticing the examples of abundance all around you and generate the energy of abundance, thereby attracting more and more examples of abundance to you. Abundant blades of grass, abundant stars in the night sky, abundant leaves on the trees...they all are ready and waiting to guide you into a state of being that only knows abundance.

When you worry or stress about the lack of something in your life you are generating the feeling, the energy of lack and so that is what you magnetize to yourself.

You can fill up your Sphere of Alignment by closing your eyes daily and generating within you the energy that you desire to feel in your life more and more. Alignment channels your attention and intention towards the vision of your desire, validates and expands the feeling of this vision realized, and then attracts to you everything you need to co-create this vision, your Unstoppable Dream, into form. The energy of alignment is depleted when you allow discordant energies to dominate your awareness. Your desires are not able to find a clear pathway of manifestation when you are preoccupying yourself with all that could go wrong or all the reasons why you don't have what you need to fulfill this desire.

Focus on the energy, the feeling, of the fruition of your desire. How will you feel when you achieve the success of your vision? Feel that now. Generate that energy from within and then welcome the energy of curiosity, wonderment and anticipation as you trust that you can only attract more and more of that same energy.

I am in harmony with the energies of my dreams.

And so it is.

 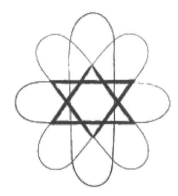 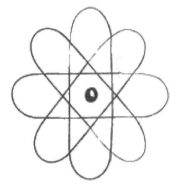

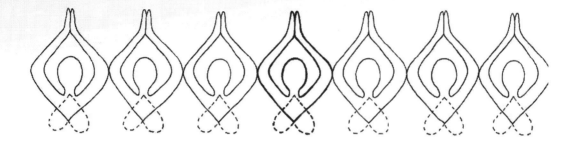

One of your most powerful manifesting energies is gratitude.
Whatever you desire to experience in your future can be
bathed now in the energy of gratitude. There is no confusion
in the energy of being grateful for something, even if it is
not being experienced now in your "present moment." When
there is this kind of coherence in your energy field, everything in the energetic dimensions responds accordingly. Not
only are you declaring your intention clearly, in a way that
leaves no room for discordance, you are already expressing
thanks to all the "powers at be" and that is a very high vibration. Thank you for being grateful.

YOUR SPHERE OF GRATITUDE— THE SHORTEST PATH TO ABUNDANCE

Today send your gratitude energy into the future.

Is there anything about your future that you worry about?

Are there any doubts or fears you have about your future? Health? Relationships? Finances?

Am I going to have enough?

Will I get sick?

Will I be alone?

Will he/she get sick?

Will I be able to take care of this house?

Will I lose touch with my kids / grandkids?

Will I ever get to...?

Will it work?

Will I lose money?

The list goes on. Right?

This is the absolute best way to replace the worry, doubt and fear with peaceful feelings, confidence, and even excited anticipation of abundance: send GRATITUDE into your future.

Imagine you are filling up your Sphere of Gratitude ahead of time.

Right now, pick one thing. Think to yourself, "I am worried that…" "I am afraid that, moving forward,…" What is it? Identify the fear or allow the first worry to come to mind.

Now reframe the worry into a positive, present moment statement. "I AM healthy." "I AM enjoying all the financial resources I need to…" "I AM in a loving relationship." "My partner and I are healthy and strong far into old age." You get it.

Write your statement below:

_____

_____

_____

_____

_____

_____

_____

_____

_____

_____

_____

_____

_____

_____

_____

Now, we are going to layer on top of that statement a gratitude-fest. Go into as much detail as you like. Expand upon all the facets of the things you are grateful for in this situation. Really put yourself there, in the future moment, feeling SO MUCH gratitude for how perfectly everything has "worked out."

I place "worked out" in quotes because the truth is that you are creating your reality. Remember everything is energy and you are a vibrational being. How can you be Unstoppable if you wrap your dreams and visions in worry, doubt and fear and believe that something outside of you has more influence than you? YOU are going to send the energy YOU want into your future experience.

I'll give you an example. After 6 years of renting after my divorce, I bought a house. I did a crazy home makeover (you can find it all on my YouTube channel), a lot of it myself. I now had a mortgage. A 30 year mortgage. 30 years! So I started to worry about being able to pay my mortgage in the future. "Sure, I am fine now. I am working away. I am still pretty young. But what about when I get older? How long can I keep this online business going? What if the internet crashes, the economy tanks...?" You get the picture.

When you find yourself in a similar pattern, the key is to hit pause on the waterfall of fearful energy and ask yourself, "What do I want?"

I imagined having all the money I needed to pay for the house and to keep up repairs. Then, I looked out at my garage / future studio. And I began sending gratitude into my future.

"I AM so grateful that I could pay for all the help I needed to renovate the garage into the studio."

"I AM so grateful to be writing this check to the bank. ...to the contractor." I would imagine myself writing checks and overflowing with gratitude as I did it.

Then, I allowed myself a walk around my house in my mind's eye. "I AM so grateful for how my house looks. ...the gardens. ...the master suite addition. I AM so grateful to have such an awesome place to live. I AM so grateful for all the friends who come to visit. ...all the wonderful contractors and other help I receive. I AM grateful!"

Now my energy is VERY different around my future house situation. I am excited—AND have started work on the studio with help from two awesome contractors!

<< Today, as I am reading for final edits I have to share this update! I now have a 15 year mortgage and was able to pay a nice chunk of cash into the mortgage when I refinanced. I am paying the same amount each month, but with only 15 years to go. The studio is complete, including a new roof! Each time I wrote a check to the contractor who helped me I repeated, "I am grateful, I am grateful..." over and over in my head. Please send gratitude into your future! It works! >>

I imagine living actively, powerfully, vibrantly until my 90th birthday and then lying down to go to sleep and transitioning out of this body with grace and ease. "I AM so grateful for my health and I AM so grateful for my peaceful and smooth transition." I really do this.

Sometimes I imagine I am shooting gratitude bombs into my future timelines, sometimes without specific targets. Just sending gratitude.

"I AM so grateful my kids are each involved in their passion and supported by loving, supportive partners!"

"I AM so grateful for all the ways our world has become a more kind, loving, compassionate place to live. Humanity is united. Peace has come to every country, every tribe and continent. I AM so grateful for the way we now care for the environment. I AM so grateful we are all living in a world guided by love, not fear. I AM grateful."

See how easy this is? Can you feel the shift even reading these words?

Now, go back to your statement that you wrote above—or go back and write it now. Create your own gratitude-fest. List below ALL the things you are grateful for around this future experience. Ready. Set. Go. "I AM grateful that...

I AM grateful...

And so it is.

You have allies all around you that want to help you amplify the energy of presence. As a human, it is inherently challenging to cultivate present moment experiences because caring for and maintaining your physical self requires planning ahead and pulling from what you've learned in the past. And you are both physical and non-physical. Your non-physical self requires regular moments of presence in order to cultivate the wisdom and perspective needed to live fully and at a high vibration. Mother eARTh is an ally and she wants to support your Sphere of Presence in three ways: through her physical manifestations, her visual manifestations, and her energetic manifestations. You are opening up now to this greatest of allies along your journey to Unstoppableness.

YOUR SPHERE OF PRESENCE— CULTIVATE PRESENCE NOW

Today you remember how to cultivate your vibrational wellness with the energy of presence.

You know the frenetic energy of taking care of your daily activities. Work, the commute, cleaning, cooking, fixing, communicating, paying bills, planning ahead...

Within the spheres of each of these activities is a center point. This center is presence. You are now going to remember that you can choose to operate without this center, and it will be as if you are a dot pinging back and forth within your sphere of physical activity in a random, frenetic way. Or you can choose to perform each activity from your center, and the potential to move through your daily tasks anchored in the present moment becomes possible.

The secret is to regularly tap into the energy of presence throughout your day.

Here are the ways Mother eARTh wants to help you:

The first way is to bring to your mind a physical element of her landscape, how she manifests in physical form. It could be a tree, a river, the ocean, a mountain...

This aspect of Mother eARTh contains a blueprint that can help you in the now. The tree wants to remind you to sink your roots into the present moment and that from there you can reach out into the field of pure potential. The river wants to remind you that life flows, change is constant, and right NOW you can resist the current, fighting the inevitable or go with the flow. The ocean wants to reassure you with her ebb and her flow. She reminds you that you are at once the wave and the entire ocean. In the present moment the ocean can open you up to the breadth and depth of what is available to you. The mountain can help you to feel strong and secure and remind you how to magnetize to yourself whatever you need to create your day from your highest vibration.

The second way Mother eARTh wants to offer you support is through images or symbols that you can use as a yantra, a visual mantra, to help you to focus your attention on the right now. You can allow an image to come to mind or you can notice when there is a symbol or image being offered to you; perhaps an animal that appears in an unusual way or more than once in a short period of time, or a flower or shape that captures your attention in any way. In a moment you can bring this image into your mind's eye, allowing it to distract your past future awareness into the present moment, and receive guidance that will serve your highest expression. Does the flower want you to risk your own bloom or open to receive more light or to serve others from a place of beauty? Does the spiral want to remind you that you are on a journey of learning, growth and expansion and help you to relax as you cross your next threshold? Perhaps a leaf conjures the energy of being both an individual and part of, one with, the collective. Allow whatever comes to mind, within your activity of working, cleaning, fixing... to replenish your Sphere of Presence.

Thirdly, there is the energy radiating from every blade of grass in your yard or every grain of sand on the beach. Feeling overwhelmed? You can go and sit against a tree and receive its particular frequency. Feeling upset by something that just happened? Go to or imagine you are walking beside a river, allowing the flow to carry your frustrations away or reminding you that "this too shall pass." You can pick up a rock, when you are feeling small and alone, and connect to HOW OLD that rock is. Even the smallest pebble can help you to put life into a perspective that serves you in an instant.

Imagine now that you are walking along a mountain path. You see the towering trees on either side of you and you feel yourself gradually walking uphill. In the distance you notice the light growing brighter and soon the forest path opens into a large meadow surrounded by a ring of mountain peaks. In the center of the meadow is a large, rounded rock. You walk to it and understand that you are meant to sit on the rock. You cross your legs, straighten your spine and close your eyes. You feel the sunlight on your body, the wind caressing your skin. You sense the openness and the protective energies of this space. You absorb the energy of harmony, each eARTh element supporting and receiving from each other. You can feel your body growing heavier, like the rock, sinking into the support provided by Mother eARTh underneath you. You simultaneously feel the lightness of your being, floating up into the illuminated sky, expanding into and becoming one with every gust of wind, every bit of soil, rock, water, flora and fauna. You understand now that you are as much a part of nature as any other element. Mother eARTh exists to nurture and cultivate your life, your expression, your creativity and your vibrational wellness. She is your ally. Breathe this energy of love and support into your heart. Connect to all the ways Mother eARTh's energy is woven into the fabric of your daily life. The wood structure of your home, the food you buy and prepare, the paper you work with the energy that flows from her natural resources. Connect to the wide open meadows and rings of mountaintops within you and within your life experiences. Offer gratitude to the way in which Mother eARTh is ministering to your heART right NOW. The part contains the whole. Within the present moment entire worlds exist. You are your center. You in the present moment. You creating dreams into reality.

And so it is.

Imagine you are sitting on the edge of the ocean. You can hear the waves in front of you, crashing onto the shore. Water meets land, then recedes. Then, another crash. You can feel the surge of energy as the wave crests and spills over onto itself, the white froth seeing how far onto land it can make it before being sucked back into the void that is the ocean. There is a building of energy, a release, a surge and then a retreat. Feel the waves inside of you. Hear them with your subtle self. Remember the ebbs and flows of all of life. The wave is the wave. The wave is also the ocean. The two are inseparable, yet distinct. It is the ups and downs that create the wave, that move it forward and then call it back into itself. In that same way your life and the events within it have an ebb and a flow, a high point and a low point, a time of moving ahead and a time of retreating back into itself. This flow of energy, up and down, in and out, round and round, is how your life evolves itself. It is within the dance of polarity that you learn and that you yearn. Both create movement, change and clarity. When you learn to flow with this truth you harness the power of harmony. You are in harmony. You are your most YOU. And that is as it should be.

CREATING IN HARMONY WITH POLARITY

Today you activate an entirely new state of flow.

In the summer of 2020, I was called to create an online program for Green Tara, the Buddhist Goddess of compassion and liberation. I thought I was going to host a special edition of my Buddha Painting program until Tara so clearly gave me my marching orders, "Paint the feminine Buddha. I have 21 aspects. Let's create together." In preparation, I got to revisit one of the creation stories of Green Tara, or Tara- there are multiple creation stories and this is the one I love the most, told with some creative license.

Millions of years ago, in a far away dimension, Tara was a princess named Wisdom Moon. Wisdom Moon was so radiant on her path to enlightenment that she attracted the attention of some Buddhist monks who journeyed to witness this light that they perceived from a distance. Imagine how she must have felt when the monks were announced. Excited? Proud? Joyful? The monks were clearly impressed with her level of consciousness and the truth of her enlightenment, but they were shocked to discover that the source of this light was female. After acknowledging her mastery, they (I imagine somewhat awkwardly) suggested that she hurry up and reincarnate as a man. She couldn't possibly proceed along her illuminated path as a woman. What!? She reminded them of a tenet of Buddhism that consciousness was beyond gender. And then (I imagine fiercely, yet princess-like) vowed in front of them to NEVER come back in the body of a man and that she would stay in the body of a woman, close to humanity, until all sentient beings were awakened. Tara was born!

Her story illustrates polarity in action and in harmony with the greater good. Polarity was created in the discordant opinions of the monks and Wisdom Moon. The creative result was a Goddess of Compassion and Liberation who has now been worshipped and followed for thousands of years and is still present to support you on your highest path. Without the polarity of that encounter, Tara might never have been.

Likewise, there is polarity at work in your life that is probably uncomfortable or challenging and it is a creative force intending to create a level of movement that will guide you into your next highest personal expression.

Polarity is creative. It is how life moves and expands, evolves and grows. It is within the muck of the tension of a situation that you are forced to dig deeper, to change and transform, to develop greater self-love or compassion. Your highest self dances in harmony with polarity to ensure your noblest intentions for this lifetime are met. You are remembering this now so you can flow with the ups and downs, the ebbs and the flows, the times of abundance and the times that feel more defined by scarcity. It is where you learn who you truly are and who you are not.

In hindsight, I consciously harnessed the potential of polarity to call in this teaching.

It was December 30th, 2018, my first New Year in my new house. Buying my house was my most recent unstoppable dream come true. Now that it had come to fruition, I was curious and wanted to open up to what was wanting to come through me next. What vision would inspire my next chapter?

I had read from multiple sources how the ancient shamans of Ireland were the poets and they often spent 24 hours in a completely dark hut, emerging from the darkness to write what was considered the most potent and transformational poetry.

I thought to myself, "How much more powerful to paint after being in the dark?"

At 10:00a on December 30th, I put on a sleep mask and didn't take it off until 6:00a the next morning. I wanted to begin my painting the next morning while it was still dark outside.

During that 20 hours of darkness I meditated and dreamed. During one of my first meditations, I saw the sacred geometry that is Metatron's Cube in my mind's eye. My meditation went instantly deeper and I was given the understanding that sacred geometry can accelerate and deepen our meditation practice. I was shown then that it is a "bridge" of sorts between the logical, thinking mind and the intuitive, creative mind. I understood that Metatron's Cube was a clue into what I was being called to "dream into reality" next.

So, it was within the darkness that I could "see" my next steps.

The darkness, the void, the spaciousness... is where you can connect to what is possible for you. This is why the book cover is black. Within the dark you can experience illumination. Consciously choosing to create experiences of contrast can accelerate the pace at which you can receive and then manifest your Unstoppable Dream.

I chose to enter into sustained darkness so I could see what was next. I dove underneath the surface to see what wanted to rise.

Today, relax into the ocean that is your life. It is vast, deep, and powerful. And it takes turns building up, spilling over, lapping up onto shore, and then retreating back into the spaciousness of its true nature.

And so it is.

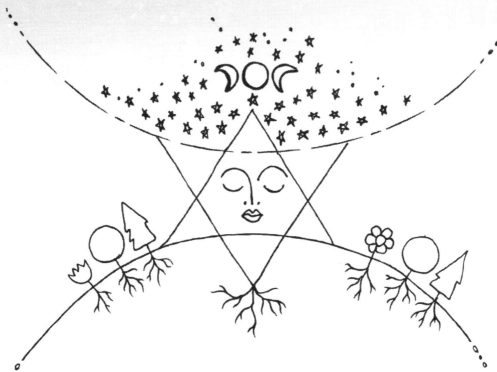

You take up more space than is defined by your skin and bones. Your field of being is expansive and we want you to tap into this sense of expansiveness more and more. You can connect with this space and feel it both as a sacred container that is you and a boundless space of possibility and security. You are being called into a new state of being that IS security, rather than looking outside of yourself for that security. You are being called into a new state of being that knows it can ONLY be safe, secure and loved because you receive the truth that you are the union of the finite and the infinite, light and matter, heaven and eARTh. You are the light and the dark, the yin and the yang, the ocean and the shore. As you remember this more and more each day, the more and more you are able to open to be the portal for the Unstoppable Dreams waiting to flow through you, in harmony and in perfect union with your heART and soul. For this we are grateful.

YOU AT THE CENTER

Today you get to feel, really feel how you are the alchemical creation of these 6 energies: love, compassion, courage, alignment, gratitude, and presence.

Wherever you are right now, begin to connect to the support underneath you. Feel how solid and secure you are here. Allow your energetic pyramid to come into focus around you. With its wide, square base and four walls reaching up to the sky, coming together in a beautiful point above you. The pyramid is a sacred geometric space and it surrounds you perfectly. You have room to stretch and move and it is cozy, like a den. You are grounded here on earth, protected and supported. Now feel into the pyramid that also surrounds you that has descended from the starry sky, the infinite void. It has descended to bless and inspire you. To remind you of your infinite nature and the wisdom you are when you remember your true infinite being. The point of this downward facing pyramid is underneath you, exactly at your center and the base of this pyramid faces to the sky, open and receptive to all the light and love.

Feel yourself here now. You are the union of light and matter. You are the energy of the divine made visible in a unique way that is celebrated by pure love. This is your truth, your hOMe.

Now you sense your Spheres of Wellness cycling around your merkaba space. They are beautiful, big, glowing orbs of light and color. Connect to each one now and fill your space with their energy.

LOVE... There is so much I love in my life. I love and respect my journey, all of it. I am loving to myself and I nurture that love within my life more and more each day. I love the trees outside, I love the sunlight, I love my cup of tea in my favorite mug, I love remembering my dreams, I love the beauty I create and surround myself with. I love my friends, my family. I am love and I honor and pursue and create love. And so it is.

COMPASSION... I am kind to myself. I allow myself time and space to learn new things, to try, to make "mistakes" and to try again. I send my self-compassion out to others, that they may also be kind to themselves. I have an easy time sending compassionate energy to those I love and to those who challenge me. I understand that everyone is trying to be loved, safe and secure. The people who challenge me the most are the ones who do not love themselves and they are not kind to themselves and I wish this for them. I am compassionate and radiate compassion. And so it is.

COURAGE... I have everything I need to take bold steps into new experiences and new aspects of me. I understand the energy of courage is here to support and prepare me for my next level of growth and learning. I often feel courageous because I am following my highest wisdom. I can trust that life is supporting me and guiding me on my highest path. Fear is really excitement. I call on my courageous self often to empower me to take leaps into the divine mystery. Because of the courage I have nurtured within me and am continuing to nurture, I know there is nothing that I can not face and manage in my life. I am strong, sovereign and confident. I am courageous. And so it is.

ALIGNMENT... I feel myself aligned with this living column of glorious white light at all times. I can feel how life is arranging itself around me to support my truest heart's desires and my most authentic self-expression. That which is no longer in alignment with my highest vibration simply slips away with grace and ease. All are served by the energy of alignment and clarity that radiates from with me. I have the courage to say no to the things that are in harmony with my Unstoppable Dream Self and to say yes to those elements that are in alignment. I am the energy of a waterfall cascading down through perfectly centered pools of luminous, life-giving water. I am the energy of the arrow shooting silently through space to its intended target. I am alignment made visible. And so it is.

GRATITUDE... I am grateful. I express my gratitude for the simplest elements in my life daily. I am grateful for all the life experiences that have brought me to this space and place today. I am grateful for all the ways I am supported and loved, from within first. I am grateful to be here now as me! I send gratitude into my future, fully knowing and trusting that my heart's desires will come to fruition because I only receive divine inspiration and surround my desires with love. I am grateful for the morning sunlight and the evening sunset. I am grateful for the smiles on the faces around me and for the wisdom and love needed to soothe the frowns. I am grateful for the nourishment I am able to provide my body and the resources I have to live comfortably and safely. I am shown so many things to be grateful for throughout my day. I am constantly bathed in gratitude and I send that energy out that all beings may also feel gratitude. And so it is.

PRESENCE... I am here now. I am moving from the present moment, informed by my past and inspired by my future and taking one step at a time as my highest path is revealed to me with so much love and light. I dance with past and future, like professional dancers gliding across a shiny floor. I have complete understanding of how I can cultivate present moments throughout my day, allowing me to take new, bolder action and to feel my unstoppableness in each moment. I know that I am supremely guided in each and every moment. I don't worry about my future or dwell in my past because I receive perfect guidance in the now. I understand that the infinite possibility, love, the divine speaks to me and inspires me in the now and we co-create new realities, informed and inspired by the past and future. I am operating from this present moment timeline and I feel more and more unstoppable each day. And so it is.

Now feel all of these energies as they have filled your merkaba space with delightful visions and energies. You are surrounded by so many things that you love and for which you are grateful. You can sense palpably that you have everything you need to take courageous steps into the unknown because you are in alignment and gentle with yourself. You are here now for a very magical reason. The space around you snaps and crackles with happy anticipation and excitement. These energies and this space feel like a beautiful cocoon or a force-field of elevated emotions that filter out any energies that are not resonant with your being. You feel protected, with a sense of invincibility because you are no longer alone or anything less than pure abundant energy. From this space you can witness lower vibrational energies, situations, relationships from a place of highest wisdom. It's like the space around you is white, puffy clouds, sparkling with sunlight and magic. This space is expansive and you feel expansive. You have everything you need exactly when you need it and you lean into that sense of trust. It feels soft and restorative. From this place you can participate in the outside world from a place of love and wisdom, radiating calm and peace everywhere you go.

You are at your center, no longer alone or isolated but connected to both your celebrated individuality and your glorious oneness. All is as it should be and everything is here to love you. Breathe this feeling and energy into your core. Breathe in all the spaciousness and exhale fulfillment. You are the Unstoppable Dream made visible.

And so it is.

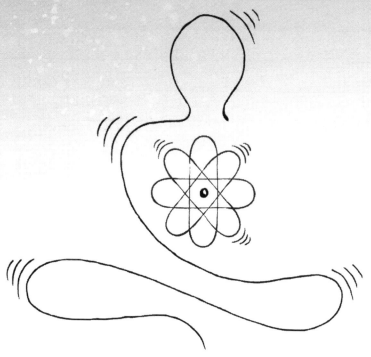

You've been in a game of hide and seek with your true Self. Your true Self hid inside your body, your physical, finite nature. You absorbed the story from your surroundings that only what you could see and touch were real and that what is subtle, intangible, and illusive is not true or real. In fact, it is the other way around. The physical dies. The subtle always is. You are a subtle energy, an infinite being first. Second, you are an individualized physical expression of the Infinite. Everything is energy. This is what unites the two YOUs. Your infinite self and your physical self are both made up of energy and vibration. The way you thrive, the way you protect yourself, the way that you access feelings of security and confidence now comes from nurturing your vibrational well-being. The higher that you maintain your vibration, the higher vibration of thoughts, experiences, and relationships you will attract. Everything is energy and like attracts like.

YOU AS A VIBRATIONAL BEING

Today you remember that your true sense of security comes from your vibration.

When I was hiking in the Himalayas, on day four of a six-day trek, I experienced "the sickness." The stomach and intestinal discomfort that comes from eating rice, lentils, and strong curries in the small villages. It came into my experience like a wave, early in the morning as we climbed the highest peak on the trek to watch the sunrise over the mountains. It slowly built in energy until mid-morning when I couldn't even carry my pack. We were hiking along a ridge, and my guide and I had switched packs, his being smaller and me being so much weaker in each moment. And, yet, we hiked, or I should say walked slowly, along this ridge with the incredible, snow-covered Himalayas on one side and a rhododendron forest on the other. A rhododendron forest! They were as big as trees, two-stories tall, and hanging on to the end of each branch were blossoms at their peak. Prayer flags woven through the branches danced the prayers of un-named souls as the wind moved up and over the ridge. I was at once in total pain and complete bliss. An awareness rippled through me, like the wind rippled through the chain of prayer flags: "I am not this body." I am BOTH physical and nonphysical. I am pure awareness, expressed through this physical body.

How could I feel SO ecstatic and also SO sick?

I was being shown that the two can exist together and separately. I am just as one as the other. And which dominated my experience? Did the waves of nausea drown out the bliss. No. Quite the opposite happened. I am consciousness and energy way before I am physical. What a gift!

What I learned from that journey is that the energies of my emotions have way more influence over my sense of well-being than the physical nature of my existence. What happens to or within the body on a physical level is not nearly as powerful an influence on my life experience as what happens from within my being on an energetic level. If you had to nurture just one, beyond the care needed to survive and function in the physical body, you choose your energetic, or vibrational well-being. You can lose everything and find everything when you follow this path or align with this truth. The external world can dish out challenges and hardships and you can still thrive when you nurture a high vibration. Instead of suffering, you learn. Instead of sacrificing, you take back power. Instead of anger, you find compassion.

You are energy first, a body second.
Your body is energy made visible.

Instead of nurturing the body, focus first on nurturing your energy. Herein lies the "fountain of youth." It is the energies of joy and happiness and compassion and peace from which you draw forth your "living waters." When you reclaim your innocence, embracing yourself as an infinite being whose number-one job is to live at as high of a vibration as possible, you let go of the expectations of others, the pressure you put on yourself to perform or achieve, and you follow the energies of joy, happiness, peace, and love. The innocence we remember here now is not about being simple or too idealistic or childlike, the way it is often perceived. It is the innocence you were born with before the world tried to take it from you.

You find joy again in the simplest things, because the vibration is highest there. You pursue those activities that raise your vibration and that get you excited because this is now the most important thing you can do to care for yourself and to feel secure and safe. Innocence comes from an inner knowing, not from something you have been taught.

Whenever life feels scary, overwhelming, or hostile, your call is simply to raise your vibration. Whether you brew a cup of tea and sit under a tree, paint a big heart, or hug your child, raise your vibration. Notice how as you become present, whatever triggered the dis-ease in your frequency dissolves into the past so that you feel better and better. From that higher frequency, you can receive the true wisdom being offered to you in that moment. Ahhhh, this is what I am being offered to learn. This is how I release this judgment or how I forgive. Whatever has happened in your external world now has to match your higher vibration and you can see it clearly, through NEW eyes... through innocence.

You are pure light energy.

You are vibration.

Everything in your experience is energy and vibration.

You surround yourself and generate from within high vibrations, and each day your life transforms to align with your vibration.

Your 401k just became 401 hertz.

The way you "insure" your happiness now and in the future is by investing in those things, activities, relationships, and ideas that are high vibration.

You are now the master of your own being. You are Unstoppable.

And so it is.

You learned how to be a good human in a culture that sees itself as a collection of individuals, separate from each other, from nature, and from the Infinite. You have to work to achieve and produce to prove your worth. You have judged yourself based on external factors and, since this pattern is inherently false, it has led to mass feelings of unworthiness.

Now you are remembering that you are the expression of part of a spectrum of energy, of light. You exist only as an interconnected being, part of a complex web of potential. You are not a single point; you are the point, all the points, completely indivisible from all that is. When you receive those powerful inspirations and visions of something that you feel deeply is meant to be experienced in your point of the spectrum, you remember that they have been given to you to midwife into your physical reality. You create these dreams into reality, not as an individual, but as part of the infinite whole with the full cooperation and co-creative energies of all that is, was, and will be. Go forth and birth your dreams, for they are our dreams, too.

YOU ARE THE UNSTOPPABLE DREAM

Are you ready to own your unstoppableness?

Take a deep breath and allow it to fill your entire core. Now exhale completely. Remember that you are inhaling the wind. You are inhaling wind that has circumnavigated the globe millions if not trillions of times. You are inhaling wind that has been around the world and that has been created by the trees and oceans and flora from Amazonian jungles to deep in the Pacific Ocean. There is no separation between your life and the life of Mother eARTh. Likewise, Mother eARTh is held in an orbit that is a delicate balance of forces that extend farther than the mind can even comprehend, all the forces harmonizing in perfect balance to create life on this planet.

You are inseparable from this spaciousness outside of you.

Within you, deep down on a micro level, you are pure energy. And if you could see yourself as pure energy, you would lose yourself because you could not tell where your body ended and the space and objects surrounding you began. From this place an idea, an emotion, and a large sofa, would all appear as energy. What is usually perceived as solid dissolves into this energetic space, and what is usually perceived as intangible, like ideas or visions, become as real as the sofa.

Your Unstoppable Dream has been circulating in this energetic realm, waiting for someone who is in alignment energetically to claim it and provide a channel for it to be experienced in this world. You become unstoppable when you recognize the continuity, rather than separation, of this creative process and simply open up to receive the inspiration and play the role of organizing the on-the-ground energies to facilitate its realization. You are the gardener being offered the tomato seed.

Instead of figuring things out, you watch for the clues. The synchronicities and coincidences will line up, when you stay open, to assist you in ushering this dream into reality and into your experience. "When the student is ready, the teacher appears." This principle holds true in all aspects of this co-creative process. Whatever you need will be provided. Patience, trust, and the ability to stay present, are necessary qualities that you bring to the process so that you do not abandon your dream before the elements can be aligned to achieve the fruition of your Unstoppable Dream. The only way your dream loses its unstoppableness is if you stop.

Breathe in the energy of curiosity right now. Breathe in and feel the energy of excitement, wonder, and anticipation. Accept this divine partnership between you and the infinite field of possibility and allow yourself the time, energy, and space to nurture and hold space for the Unstoppable Dream waiting, ready and willing to come through you.

Develop a new sensitivity to how you may have a pattern of filtering out the possibility. Your logical mind may kick in and begin to dictate a long list of improbabilities and risks connected to your partnership with your Unstoppable Dream. You may get ahead of yourself and start planning how this dream is going to proceed, and when the dream flows a different direction you misinterpret it as going wrong or not working. You abandon the creative process because it's not going the way you think it should, or it's not happening according to your timeline, and your Unstoppable Dream is abandoned.

You shift this pattern by connecting back to you as part of the whole. This dream is not coming through you for you. It is wanting to be expressed and experienced in this reality to benefit all beings. The energy of one human realizing their Unstoppable Dream, the enthusiasm, excitement, love, joy, and wisdom gained along the way raise the vibration of your planet. The more people waving their hands and exclaiming, "Look at this! I never thought it would happen! It did! You can do it too! Trust! Follow your instincts! Honor your heart! Leap! Dare! Believe!" the quicker, sooner, faster humanity will experience life rooted in love rather than fear.

And so it is.

Get quiet. Listen. Your Unstoppable Dream is just on the other side of your day-to-day consciousness. It is as if you could pull back a shower curtain to see your dream there, ready and waiting, to be grasped and pulled into reality. The first step is silence. The next step is presence. The third step is obedience... to the dream. When you choose to be obedient to the dream, you become unstoppable, and the dream that you have been shown in your quiet, present moment will come to fruition. And your journey to escorting, birthing, and midwifing... this dream into the earthly plane will yield a bountiful harvest for you of wisdom, love, and courage. It's not about doing. It is about being in a state of creative receptivity and inspired action. Together, we've got this, you and the all that is all. Are you ready? Your dream is.

Day 29

YOU RECEIVING YOUR UNSTOPPABLE DREAM

It is more simple than you *think.*

In the stillness of the present moment, you lose your past and the future cannot exist. Your limiting beliefs about what you are or aren't capable of dissolve into nothingness. You have no past that has wounded you, and you have no future to plan. You are open and receptive. You are able to receive levels of communication, insight, and wisdom that can only flow through the present and that get filtered out in the do-do-DO energy of your daily routine. From this place of quiet and presence, you will receive your Unstoppable Dream.

Nature is your ally in this creative process. Mother eARTh is generating powerful frequencies in her forests and rivers, mountains and meadows, wilderness and backyards, to align you with the energies needed to perceive what is wanting to come through you.

The creative arts is another ally. Music, dance, colors, and symbols bring you present and get you out of your mind and into your heart. Both Mother eARTh and the creative arts are the creative energy that will fuel your unstoppable journey.

Receiving your Unstoppable Dream is like embarking on a travel adventure. You will visit new places and spaces and learn more about your world and your role within it. You will be challenged; the opportunity to rise above what you thought was available to you up until now will be a partner on this journey. You will be forever changed, and your sense of being will expand as you accept the call. Ideas you picked up in your past around what is possible or not will be replaced with a new confidence in all that is available to you. You will lean into the mystery, trusting that what is coming through you is bigger than you and is here to serve a bigger purpose than meets the eye. Your Unstoppable Dream is a call to adventure; are you ready to live a hero's journey?

If so, then surrender.

Lay down your "I can'ts," "shoulds" and "have to's." Abandon your "I'm not's" and "I could never...." Choose to dance with the energies of miracles. Follow the breadcrumbs. The teachers will appear. The allies will reveal themselves. The answers to your questions will be delivered to you. Stay open. Receive. Trust. And take it one step at a time.

One step at a time.

Every Unstoppable Dream begins with a single step.

Together, we will defy what has been thought possible.

Together we will create more and more love, compassion, courage, alignment, gratitude, and presence. And from this vibrational state of being, the world will shift out of the age of fear and into the age of love.

And so it is.

We want you to spend more time looking at the in-between spaces. The quiet moments, the space between things. Within these pauses and clearings, your knowing will arise. Your Unstoppable Dream Self exists in the nothingness, not in the land of what already is. Attune your awareness to these voids, the portals through which possibility makes itself visible.

YOUR DAILY PRACTICE

Today, ask yourself, "What if..."

These two words illuminate the space.

These two words engage your imagination. You may have been taught that imagination isn't real or that it distracts you from "real life." The truth is that your imagination is the space, the nothingness, that creates space for newness. If you can imagine it, you can experience it.

What if...

Each day, start a journal entry or muse as you walk outside, with these two words. And just pay attention. Take note. In the space following those two words, at the perfect moment, you will meet your next Unstoppable Dream.

Then, once you feel that resonance, the excitement and the sizzle, ask yourself again, "What if...?"

This will keep you open. Your Unstoppable Dream will be affirmed or not in the two days following its reception. You don't have to DO anything. Keep asking "What if..." and then watch for the clues or for the pathway to begin to reveal itself.

Your daily practice is to nurture this energy of "What if..." and to maintain your vibrational being at a high enough frequency, supported and bathed in the energies of love, compassion, courage, alignment, gratitude, and presence, so that you are flowing with the creative currents of possibility.

If you feel the doubt, scan your vibrational space. Which Sphere of Wellness calls to you? Meditate on that. When in doubt, start immersing yourself in all for which you are grateful. Or allow your eyes to search out something you love. Create the opportunity to experience the vibration of presence. When in doubt, remember union. Enter into your merkaba, held by the love of below and above and feel the energies swirling around you in their luminescent spheres, bathing you in the blended light of love, compassion, courage, alignment, gratitude, and presence.

Look out your window for the wind dancing with the leaves. Breathe it in. Allow the truth that which you cannot see—the wind—is also what gives you life. The most important things are often invisible. It is the subtle forces that guide life on this planet. You are opening up more and more each day to all the ways you can harmonize with and harness these subtle forces.

What if...?

The doorway through which you meet your Unstoppable Dream is inherently empty space. You open more and more each day to this emptiness, and through that portal, you become unstoppable.

Closure

Wow! If you had handed me this book back in 1996 and told me that I would write this, I would have thought you were smoking something!

I know that every word is here as an offering.

All I can feel as I imagine into the future trajectory of this book is that right now all that matters is what YOU do next. Next, like in the next minute or hour or two days. What if this isn't a book as much as a signal?

The time is now.

You have been looking, searching... for YOU.

You are the Dream Made Visible. As much as you cherish your child, grandmother, or lover, you are cherished a million times more. You remembering is a dream come to fruition, and now you have the opportunity to co-create dreams until they are visible and celebrated!

This awareness had been put into "sleep mode" for multiple centuries, and now it has been awakened. You are awake. "You can't un-ring the bell," as they say.

Consider yourself RUNG. You are UNSTOPPABLE. Go make your dreams visible.

And... so... it... is...

Use **#iamthedreammadevisible** to share your journey and your milestones with me and be sure to check out the companion online course to this book at **WhitneyFreya.com.**

About the Author
WHITNEY FREYA

Whitney Freya is a modern day mystic and an expert in Inspired Living, providing practical tools and practices that free your mind from limitations and scarcity to create more in your life that lights you up from the inside out.

She is the author of *Rise Above, Free Your Mind One Brush Stroke at a Time* and *The Artist Within, A Guide to Becoming Creatively Fit.* She is Chief Muse at WhitneyFreyaStudio.com and leads online experiences to inspire you to imagine into your highest personal expression and create it into your reality.

Her Creatively Fit Coaches are a worldwide foce of creative possibility. She lives in NE Oregon and is either flying her paraglider or skiing around the mountains there, if she is not in her studio.

Her three children are all off creating their own Unstoppable Dreams into reality. Learn more and connect at **WhitneyFreya.com.**

Additional books by Flower of Life Press

Rise Above: Free Your Mind One Brushstroke at a Time

The New Feminine Evolutionary: Embody Presence—Become the Change

Pioneering the Path to Prosperity: Discover the Power of True Wealth and Abundance

Sacred Body Wisdom: Igniting the Flame of Our Divine Humanity

Set Sail: Shine Your Radiance, Activate Your Ascension, Ignite Your Income, Live Your Legacy

Practice: Wisdom from the Downward Dog

Sisterhood of the Mindful Goddess: How to Remove Obstacles, Activate Your Gifts, and Become Your Own Superhero

Sovereign Unto Herself: Release Co-Dependencies and Claim Your Authentic Power

Path of the Priestess: Discover Your Divine Purpose

Sacred Call of the Ancient Priestess: Birthing a New Feminine Archetype

Menopause Mavens: Master the Mystery of Menopause

The Power of Essential Oils: Create Positive Transformation in Your Well-Being, Business, and Life

Self-Made Wellionaire: Get Off Your Ass(et), Reclaim Your Health, and Feel Like a Million Bucks

Emerge: 7 Steps to Transformation (No matter what life throws at you!)

Oms From the Mat: Breathe, Move, and Awaken to the Power of Yoga

Oms From the Heart: Open Your Heart to the Power of Yoga

The Four Tenets of Love: Open, Activate, and Inspire Your Life's Path

The Fire-Driven Life: Ignite the Fire of Self-Worth, Health, and Happiness with a Plant-Based Diet

Becoming Enough: A Heroine's Journey to the Already Perfect Self

The Caregiving Journey: Information. Guidance. Inspiration.

Plant-based Vegan & Gluten-free Cooking with Essential Oils

Stone Warrior: Confronting Life's Dark Challenges with Stone Art and Meditation

Sacred Reunion: Love Poems to the Masculine & Feminine—An Anthology

www.floweroflifepress.com
FREE TRAINING: www.bestsellerpriestess.com/bestseller-priestess

Made in the USA
Middletown, DE
25 September 2021